I0309175

C-1079 CAREER EXAMINATION SERIES

This is your PASSBOOK for...

Administrative Officer

Test Preparation Study Guide
Questions & Answers

NLC®
NATIONAL LEARNING CORPORATION®

National Learning Corporation

212 Michael Drive, Syosset, NY 11791
(516) 921-8888 • www.passbooks.com
E-mail: info@passbooks.com

PUBLISHED IN THE UNITED STATES OF AMERICA

PASSBOOK® SERIES

THE *PASSBOOK® SERIES* has been created to prepare applicants and candidates for the ultimate academic battlefield – the examination room.

At some time in our lives, each and every one of us may be required to take an examination – for validation, matriculation, admission, qualification, registration, certification, or licensure.

Based on the assumption that every applicant or candidate has met the basic formal educational standards, has taken the required number of courses, and read the necessary texts, the *PASSBOOK® SERIES* furnishes the one special preparation which may assure passing with confidence, instead of failing with insecurity. Examination questions – together with answers – are furnished as the basic vehicle for study so that the mysteries of the examination and its compounding difficulties may be eliminated or diminished by a sure method.

This book is meant to help you pass your examination provided that you qualify and are serious in your objective.

The entire field is reviewed through the huge store of content information which is succinctly presented through a provocative and challenging approach – the question-and-answer method.

A climate of success is established by furnishing the correct answers at the end of each test.

You soon learn to recognize types of questions, forms of questions, and patterns of questioning. You may even begin to anticipate expected outcomes.

You perceive that many questions are repeated or adapted so that you can gain acute insights, which may enable you to score many sure points.

You learn how to confront new questions, or types of questions, and to attack them confidently and work out the correct answers.

You note objectives and emphases, and recognize pitfalls and dangers, so that you may make positive educational adjustments.

Moreover, you are kept fully informed in relation to new concepts, methods, practices, and directions in the field.

You discover that you are actually taking the examination all the time: you are preparing for the examination by "taking" an examination, not by reading extraneous and/or supererogatory textbooks.

In short, this PASSBOOK®, used directedly, should be an important factor in helping you to pass your test.

ADMINISTRATIVE OFFICER

DUTIES

As an Administrative Officer, you would direct a combination of business administration and fiscal activities for a department. Performs highly responsible administrative work in directing a major departmental program, or performing important management functions of comparable responsibility. The Administrative Officer is directly responsible for all administrative activities, including payroll, purchasing, accounting, budgeting, communications, office space management, inventory management, records management, mail and supply, reproduction, filing, and technical supervision of these same administrative duties by clerical forces in management field offices. The Administrative Officer is also frequently called upon to coordinate activities between other program operations in special problem situations.

This is office management work supervising the provision of administrative services for a small department or a large division of an operating department with specific services provided to include the preparation and control of the budget, supervising, planning, assigning, coordinating, and reviewing the activities of a subordinate clerical and technical staff engaged in the purchase of goods and services, and maintenance of a variety of divisional and/or departmental reports and records. And employee in this class collects and compiles data for preliminary budget preparation and prepares justification for modifications in expenditures. In addition to the above responsibilities, work may include preparation of the capital budget, supervision of the department's personnel function, and may supervise through subordinate supervisors. This class is differentiated from the next lower level supervisory class by the specific responsibility for preparation and control of a departmental or an operations divisional budget and the purchase of goods and services. A significant aspect of the work is supervising a staff of clerical and technical personnel engaged in varied office management functions in support of divisional or departmental requirements. Work is performed under the direction of an administrative superior.

SCOPE OF THE EXAMINATION

The multiple-choice written test will cover knowledge, skills and/or abilities in such areas as:

1. Administration;
2. Supervision;
3. Educating and interacting with the public;
4. Preparation of written material; and
5. Understanding and interpreting written material.

HOW TO TAKE A TEST

I. YOU MUST PASS AN EXAMINATION

A. WHAT EVERY CANDIDATE SHOULD KNOW

Examination applicants often ask us for help in preparing for the written test. What can I study in advance? What kinds of questions will be asked? How will the test be given? How will the papers be graded?

As an applicant for a civil service examination, you may be wondering about some of these things. Our purpose here is to suggest effective methods of advance study and to describe civil service examinations.

Your chances for success on this examination can be increased if you know how to prepare. Those "pre-examination jitters" can be reduced if you know what to expect. You can even experience an adventure in good citizenship if you know why civil service exams are given.

B. WHY ARE CIVIL SERVICE EXAMINATIONS GIVEN?

Civil service examinations are important to you in two ways. As a citizen, you want public jobs filled by employees who know how to do their work. As a job seeker, you want a fair chance to compete for that job on an equal footing with other candidates. The best-known means of accomplishing this two-fold goal is the competitive examination.

Exams are widely publicized throughout the nation. They may be administered for jobs in federal, state, city, municipal, town or village governments or agencies.

Any citizen may apply, with some limitations, such as the age or residence of applicants. Your experience and education may be reviewed to see whether you meet the requirements for the particular examination. When these requirements exist, they are reasonable and applied consistently to all applicants. Thus, a competitive examination may cause you some uneasiness now, but it is your privilege and safeguard.

C. HOW ARE CIVIL SERVICE EXAMS DEVELOPED?

Examinations are carefully written by trained technicians who are specialists in the field known as "psychological measurement," in consultation with recognized authorities in the field of work that the test will cover. These experts recommend the subject matter areas or skills to be tested; only those knowledges or skills important to your success on the job are included. The most reliable books and source materials available are used as references. Together, the experts and technicians judge the difficulty level of the questions.

Test technicians know how to phrase questions so that the problem is clearly stated. Their ethics do not permit "trick" or "catch" questions. Questions may have been tried out on sample groups, or subjected to statistical analysis, to determine their usefulness.

Written tests are often used in combination with performance tests, ratings of training and experience, and oral interviews. All of these measures combine to form the best-known means of finding the right person for the right job.

II. HOW TO PASS THE WRITTEN TEST

A. NATURE OF THE EXAMINATION

To prepare intelligently for civil service examinations, you should know how they differ from school examinations you have taken. In school you were assigned certain definite pages to read or subjects to cover. The examination questions were quite detailed and usually emphasized memory. Civil service exams, on the other hand, try to discover your present ability to perform the duties of a position, plus your potentiality to learn these duties. In other words, a civil service exam attempts to predict how successful you will be. Questions cover such a broad area that they cannot be as minute and detailed as school exam questions.

In the public service similar kinds of work, or positions, are grouped together in one "class." This process is known as *position-classification.* All the positions in a class are paid according to the salary range for that class. One class title covers all of these positions, and they are all tested by the same examination.

B. FOUR BASIC STEPS

1) Study the announcement

How, then, can you know what subjects to study? Our best answer is: "Learn as much as possible about the class of positions for which you've applied." The exam will test the knowledge, skills and abilities needed to do the work.

Your most valuable source of information about the position you want is the official exam announcement. This announcement lists the training and experience qualifications. Check these standards and apply only if you come reasonably close to meeting them.

The brief description of the position in the examination announcement offers some clues to the subjects which will be tested. Think about the job itself. Review the duties in your mind. Can you perform them, or are there some in which you are rusty? Fill in the blank spots in your preparation.

Many jurisdictions preview the written test in the exam announcement by including a section called "Knowledge and Abilities Required," "Scope of the Examination," or some similar heading. Here you will find out specifically what fields will be tested.

2) Review your own background

Once you learn in general what the position is all about, and what you need to know to do the work, ask yourself which subjects you already know fairly well and which need improvement. You may wonder whether to concentrate on improving your strong areas or on building some background in your fields of weakness. When the announcement has specified "some knowledge" or "considerable knowledge," or has used adjectives like "beginning principles of..." or "advanced ... methods," you can get a clue as to the number and difficulty of questions to be asked in any given field. More questions, and hence broader coverage, would be included for those subjects which are more important in the work. Now weigh your strengths and weaknesses against the job requirements and prepare accordingly.

3) Determine the level of the position

Another way to tell how intensively you should prepare is to understand the level of the job for which you are applying. Is it the entering level? In other words, is this the position in which beginners in a field of work are hired? Or is it an intermediate or advanced level? Sometimes this is indicated by such words as "Junior" or "Senior" in the class title. Other jurisdictions use Roman numerals to designate the level – Clerk I, Clerk II, for example. The word "Supervisor" sometimes appears in the title. If the level is not indicated by the title, check the description of duties. Will you be working under very close supervision, or will you have responsibility for independent decisions in this work?

4) Choose appropriate study materials

Now that you know the subjects to be examined and the relative amount of each subject to be covered, you can choose suitable study materials. For beginning level jobs, or even advanced ones, if you have a pronounced weakness in some aspect of your training, read a modern, standard textbook in that field. Be sure it is up to date and has general coverage. Such books are normally available at your library, and the librarian will be glad to help you locate one. For entry-level positions, questions of appropriate difficulty are chosen – neither highly advanced questions, nor those too simple. Such questions require careful thought but not advanced training.

If the position for which you are applying is technical or advanced, you will read more advanced, specialized material. If you are already familiar with the basic principles of your field, elementary textbooks would waste your time. Concentrate on advanced textbooks and technical periodicals. Think through the concepts and review difficult problems in your field.

These are all general sources. You can get more ideas on your own initiative, following these leads. For example, training manuals and publications of the government agency which employs workers in your field can be useful, particularly for technical and professional positions. A letter or visit to the government department involved may result in more specific study suggestions, and certainly will provide you with a more definite idea of the exact nature of the position you are seeking.

III. KINDS OF TESTS

Tests are used for purposes other than measuring knowledge and ability to perform specified duties. For some positions, it is equally important to test ability to make adjustments to new situations or to profit from training. In others, basic mental abilities not dependent on information are essential. Questions which test these things may not appear as pertinent to the duties of the position as those which test for knowledge and information. Yet they are often highly important parts of a fair examination. For very general questions, it is almost impossible to help you direct your study efforts. What we can do is to point out some of the more common of these general abilities needed in public service positions and describe some typical questions.

1) General information

Broad, general information has been found useful for predicting job success in some kinds of work. This is tested in a variety of ways, from vocabulary lists to questions about current events. Basic background in some field of work, such as sociology or economics, may be sampled in a group of questions. Often these are principles which have become familiar to most persons through exposure rather than through formal training. It is difficult to advise you how to study for these questions; being alert to the world around you is our best suggestion.

2) Verbal ability

An example of an ability needed in many positions is verbal or language ability. Verbal ability is, in brief, the ability to use and understand words. Vocabulary and grammar tests are typical measures of this ability. Reading comprehension or paragraph interpretation questions are common in many kinds of civil service tests. You are given a paragraph of written material and asked to find its central meaning.

3) Numerical ability

Number skills can be tested by the familiar arithmetic problem, by checking paired lists of numbers to see which are alike and which are different, or by interpreting charts and graphs. In the latter test, a graph may be printed in the test booklet which you are asked to use as the basis for answering questions.

4) Observation

A popular test for law-enforcement positions is the observation test. A picture is shown to you for several minutes, then taken away. Questions about the picture test your ability to observe both details and larger elements.

5) Following directions

In many positions in the public service, the employee must be able to carry out written instructions dependably and accurately. You may be given a chart with several columns, each column listing a variety of information. The questions require you to carry out directions involving the information given in the chart.

6) Skills and aptitudes

Performance tests effectively measure some manual skills and aptitudes. When the skill is one in which you are trained, such as typing or shorthand, you can practice. These tests are often very much like those given in business school or high school courses. For many of the other skills and aptitudes, however, no short-time preparation can be made. Skills and abilities natural to you or that you have developed throughout your lifetime are being tested.

Many of the general questions just described provide all the data needed to answer the questions and ask you to use your reasoning ability to find the answers. Your best preparation for these tests, as well as for tests of facts and ideas, is to be at your physical and mental best. You, no doubt, have your own methods of getting into an exam-taking mood and keeping "in shape." The next section lists some ideas on this subject.

IV. KINDS OF QUESTIONS

Only rarely is the "essay" question, which you answer in narrative form, used in civil service tests. Civil service tests are usually of the short-answer type. Full instructions for answering these questions will be given to you at the examination. But in case this is your first experience with short-answer questions and separate answer sheets, here is what you need to know:

1) Multiple-choice Questions

Most popular of the short-answer questions is the "multiple choice" or "best answer" question. It can be used, for example, to test for factual knowledge, ability to solve problems or judgment in meeting situations found at work.

A multiple-choice question is normally one of three types—

- It can begin with an incomplete statement followed by several possible endings. You are to find the one ending which *best* completes the statement, although some of the others may not be entirely wrong.
- It can also be a complete statement in the form of a question which is answered by choosing one of the statements listed.

- It can be in the form of a problem – again you select the best answer.

Here is an example of a multiple-choice question with a discussion which should give you some clues as to the method for choosing the right answer:

When an employee has a complaint about his assignment, the action which will *best* help him overcome his difficulty is to

A. discuss his difficulty with his coworkers
B. take the problem to the head of the organization
C. take the problem to the person who gave him the assignment
D. say nothing to anyone about his complaint

In answering this question, you should study each of the choices to find which is best. Consider choice "A" – Certainly an employee may discuss his complaint with fellow employees, but no change or improvement can result, and the complaint remains unresolved. Choice "B" is a poor choice since the head of the organization probably does not know what assignment you have been given, and taking your problem to him is known as "going over the head" of the supervisor. The supervisor, or person who made the assignment, is the person who can clarify it or correct any injustice. Choice "C" is, therefore, correct. To say nothing, as in choice "D," is unwise. Supervisors have and interest in knowing the problems employees are facing, and the employee is seeking a solution to his problem.

2) True/False Questions

The "true/false" or "right/wrong" form of question is sometimes used. Here a complete statement is given. Your job is to decide whether the statement is right or wrong.

SAMPLE: A roaming cell-phone call to a nearby city costs less than a non-roaming call to a distant city.

This statement is wrong, or false, since roaming calls are more expensive.

This is not a complete list of all possible question forms, although most of the others are variations of these common types. You will always get complete directions for answering questions. Be sure you understand *how* to mark your answers – ask questions until you do.

V. RECORDING YOUR ANSWERS

Computer terminals are used more and more today for many different kinds of exams.

For an examination with very few applicants, you may be told to record your answers in the test booklet itself. Separate answer sheets are much more common. If this separate answer sheet is to be scored by machine – and this is often the case – it is highly important that you mark your answers correctly in order to get credit.

An electronic scoring machine is often used in civil service offices because of the speed with which papers can be scored. Machine-scored answer sheets must be marked with a pencil, which will be given to you. This pencil has a high graphite content which responds to the electronic scoring machine. As a matter of fact, stray dots may register as answers, so do not let your pencil rest on the answer sheet while you are pondering the correct answer. Also, if your pencil lead breaks or is otherwise defective, ask for another.

Since the answer sheet will be dropped in a slot in the scoring machine, be careful not to bend the corners or get the paper crumpled.

The answer sheet normally has five vertical columns of numbers, with 30 numbers to a column. These numbers correspond to the question numbers in your test booklet. After each number, going across the page are four or five pairs of dotted lines. These short dotted lines have small letters or numbers above them. The first two pairs may also have a "T" or "F" above the letters. This indicates that the first two pairs only are to be used if the questions are of the true-false type. If the questions are multiple choice, disregard the "T" and "F" and pay attention only to the small letters or numbers.

Answer your questions in the manner of the sample that follows:

32. The largest city in the United States is
    A. Washington, D.C.
    B. New York City
    C. Chicago
    D. Detroit
    E. San Francisco

1) Choose the answer you think is best. (New York City is the largest, so "B" is correct.)
2) Find the row of dotted lines numbered the same as the question you are answering. (Find row number 32)
3) Find the pair of dotted lines corresponding to the answer. (Find the pair of lines under the mark "B.")
4) Make a solid black mark between the dotted lines.

VI. BEFORE THE TEST

Common sense will help you find procedures to follow to get ready for an examination. Too many of us, however, overlook these sensible measures. Indeed, nervousness and fatigue have been found to be the most serious reasons why applicants fail to do their best on civil service tests. Here is a list of reminders:

- Begin your preparation early – Don't wait until the last minute to go scurrying around for books and materials or to find out what the position is all about.
- Prepare continuously – An hour a night for a week is better than an all-night cram session. This has been definitely established. What is more, a night a week for a month will return better dividends than crowding your study into a shorter period of time.
- Locate the place of the exam – You have been sent a notice telling you when and where to report for the examination. If the location is in a different town or otherwise unfamiliar to you, it would be well to inquire the best route and learn something about the building.
- Relax the night before the test – Allow your mind to rest. Do not study at all that night. Plan some mild recreation or diversion; then go to bed early and get a good night's sleep.
- Get up early enough to make a leisurely trip to the place for the test – This way unforeseen events, traffic snarls, unfamiliar buildings, etc. will not upset you.
- Dress comfortably – A written test is not a fashion show. You will be known by number and not by name, so wear something comfortable.

- Leave excess paraphernalia at home – Shopping bags and odd bundles will get in your way. You need bring only the items mentioned in the official notice you received; usually everything you need is provided. Do not bring reference books to the exam. They will only confuse those last minutes and be taken away from you when in the test room.
- Arrive somewhat ahead of time – If because of transportation schedules you must get there very early, bring a newspaper or magazine to take your mind off yourself while waiting.
- Locate the examination room – When you have found the proper room, you will be directed to the seat or part of the room where you will sit. Sometimes you are given a sheet of instructions to read while you are waiting. Do not fill out any forms until you are told to do so; just read them and be prepared.
- Relax and prepare to listen to the instructions
- If you have any physical problem that may keep you from doing your best, be sure to tell the test administrator. If you are sick or in poor health, you really cannot do your best on the exam. You can come back and take the test some other time.

VII. AT THE TEST

The day of the test is here and you have the test booklet in your hand. The temptation to get going is very strong. Caution! There is more to success than knowing the right answers. You must know how to identify your papers and understand variations in the type of short-answer question used in this particular examination. Follow these suggestions for maximum results from your efforts:

1) Cooperate with the monitor

The test administrator has a duty to create a situation in which you can be as much at ease as possible. He will give instructions, tell you when to begin, check to see that you are marking your answer sheet correctly, and so on. He is not there to guard you, although he will see that your competitors do not take unfair advantage. He wants to help you do your best.

2) Listen to all instructions

Don't jump the gun! Wait until you understand all directions. In most civil service tests you get more time than you need to answer the questions. So don't be in a hurry. Read each word of instructions until you clearly understand the meaning. Study the examples, listen to all announcements and follow directions. Ask questions if you do not understand what to do.

3) Identify your papers

Civil service exams are usually identified by number only. You will be assigned a number; you must not put your name on your test papers. Be sure to copy your number correctly. Since more than one exam may be given, copy your exact examination title.

4) Plan your time

Unless you are told that a test is a "speed" or "rate of work" test, speed itself is usually not important. Time enough to answer all the questions will be provided, but this does not mean that you have all day. An overall time limit has been set. Divide the total time (in minutes) by the number of questions to determine the approximate time you have for each question.

5) Do not linger over difficult questions

If you come across a difficult question, mark it with a paper clip (useful to have along) and come back to it when you have been through the booklet. One caution if you do this – be sure to skip a number on your answer sheet as well. Check often to be sure that you have not lost your place and that you are marking in the row numbered the same as the question you are answering.

6) Read the questions

Be sure you know what the question asks! Many capable people are unsuccessful because they failed to *read* the questions correctly.

7) Answer all questions

Unless you have been instructed that a penalty will be deducted for incorrect answers, it is better to guess than to omit a question.

8) Speed tests

It is often better NOT to guess on speed tests. It has been found that on timed tests people are tempted to spend the last few seconds before time is called in marking answers at random – without even reading them – in the hope of picking up a few extra points. To discourage this practice, the instructions may warn you that your score will be "corrected" for guessing. That is, a penalty will be applied. The incorrect answers will be deducted from the correct ones, or some other penalty formula will be used.

9) Review your answers

If you finish before time is called, go back to the questions you guessed or omitted to give them further thought. Review other answers if you have time.

10) Return your test materials

If you are ready to leave before others have finished or time is called, take ALL your materials to the monitor and leave quietly. Never take any test material with you. The monitor can discover whose papers are not complete, and taking a test booklet may be grounds for disqualification.

VIII. EXAMINATION TECHNIQUES

1) Read the general instructions carefully. These are usually printed on the first page of the exam booklet. As a rule, these instructions refer to the timing of the examination; the fact that you should not start work until the signal and must stop work at a signal, etc. If there are any *special* instructions, such as a choice of questions to be answered, make sure that you note this instruction carefully.

2) When you are ready to start work on the examination, that is as soon as the signal has been given, read the instructions to each question booklet, underline any key words or phrases, such as *least*, *best*, *outline*, *describe* and the like. In this way you will tend to answer as requested rather than discover on reviewing your paper that you *listed without describing*, that you selected the *worst* choice rather than the *best* choice, etc.

3) If the examination is of the objective or multiple-choice type – that is, each question will also give a series of possible answers: A, B, C or D, and you are called upon to select the best answer and write the letter next to that answer on your answer paper – it is advisable to start answering each question in turn. There may be anywhere from 50 to 100 such questions in the three or four hours allotted and you can see how much time would be taken if you read through all the questions before beginning to answer any. Furthermore, if you come across a question or group of questions which you know would be difficult to answer, it would undoubtedly affect your handling of all the other questions.

4) If the examination is of the essay type and contains but a few questions, it is a moot point as to whether you should read all the questions before starting to answer any one. Of course, if you are given a choice – say five out of seven and the like – then it is essential to read all the questions so you can eliminate the two that are most difficult. If, however, you are asked to answer all the questions, there may be danger in trying to answer the easiest one first because you may find that you will spend too much time on it. The best technique is to answer the first question, then proceed to the second, etc.

5) Time your answers. Before the exam begins, write down the time it started, then add the time allowed for the examination and write down the time it must be completed, then divide the time available somewhat as follows:
   - If 3-1/2 hours are allowed, that would be 210 minutes. If you have 80 objective-type questions, that would be an average of 2-1/2 minutes per question. Allow yourself no more than 2 minutes per question, or a total of 160 minutes, which will permit about 50 minutes to review.
   - If for the time allotment of 210 minutes there are 7 essay questions to answer, that would average about 30 minutes a question. Give yourself only 25 minutes per question so that you have about 35 minutes to review.

6) The most important instruction is to *read each question* and make sure you know what is wanted. The second most important instruction is to *time yourself properly* so that you answer every question. The third most important instruction is to *answer every question*. Guess if you have to but include something for each question. Remember that you will receive no credit for a blank and will probably receive some credit if you write something in answer to an essay question. If you guess a letter – say "B" for a multiple-choice question – you may have guessed right. If you leave a blank as an answer to a multiple-choice question, the examiners may respect your feelings but it will not add a point to your score. Some exams may penalize you for wrong answers, so in such cases *only*, you may not want to guess unless you have some basis for your answer.

7) Suggestions
   a. Objective-type questions
      1. Examine the question booklet for proper sequence of pages and questions
      2. Read all instructions carefully
      3. Skip any question which seems too difficult; return to it after all other questions have been answered
      4. Apportion your time properly; do not spend too much time on any single question or group of questions

5. Note and underline key words – *all, most, fewest, least, best, worst, same, opposite,* etc.
6. Pay particular attention to negatives
7. Note unusual option, e.g., unduly long, short, complex, different or similar in content to the body of the question
8. Observe the use of "hedging" words – *probably, may, most likely,* etc.
9. Make sure that your answer is put next to the same number as the question
10. Do not second-guess unless you have good reason to believe the second answer is definitely more correct
11. Cross out original answer if you decide another answer is more accurate; do not erase until you are ready to hand your paper in
12. Answer all questions; guess unless instructed otherwise
13. Leave time for review

b. Essay questions
1. Read each question carefully
2. Determine exactly what is wanted. Underline key words or phrases.
3. Decide on outline or paragraph answer
4. Include many different points and elements unless asked to develop any one or two points or elements
5. Show impartiality by giving pros and cons unless directed to select one side only
6. Make and write down any assumptions you find necessary to answer the questions
7. Watch your English, grammar, punctuation and choice of words
8. Time your answers; don't crowd material

8) Answering the essay question

Most essay questions can be answered by framing the specific response around several key words or ideas. Here are a few such key words or ideas:

M's: manpower, materials, methods, money, management
P's: purpose, program, policy, plan, procedure, practice, problems, pitfalls, personnel, public relations

a. Six basic steps in handling problems:
1. Preliminary plan and background development
2. Collect information, data and facts
3. Analyze and interpret information, data and facts
4. Analyze and develop solutions as well as make recommendations
5. Prepare report and sell recommendations
6. Install recommendations and follow up effectiveness

b. Pitfalls to avoid
1. *Taking things for granted* – A statement of the situation does not necessarily imply that each of the elements is necessarily true; for example, a complaint may be invalid and biased so that all that can be taken for granted is that a complaint has been registered

2. *Considering only one side of a situation* – Wherever possible, indicate several alternatives and then point out the reasons you selected the best one
3. *Failing to indicate follow up* – Whenever your answer indicates action on your part, make certain that you will take proper follow-up action to see how successful your recommendations, procedures or actions turn out to be
4. *Taking too long in answering any single question* – Remember to time your answers properly

IX. AFTER THE TEST

Scoring procedures differ in detail among civil service jurisdictions although the general principles are the same. Whether the papers are hand-scored or graded by machine we have described, they are nearly always graded by number. That is, the person who marks the paper knows only the number – never the name – of the applicant. Not until all the papers have been graded will they be matched with names. If other tests, such as training and experience or oral interview ratings have been given, scores will be combined. Different parts of the examination usually have different weights. For example, the written test might count 60 percent of the final grade, and a rating of training and experience 40 percent. In many jurisdictions, veterans will have a certain number of points added to their grades.

After the final grade has been determined, the names are placed in grade order and an eligible list is established. There are various methods for resolving ties between those who get the same final grade – probably the most common is to place first the name of the person whose application was received first. Job offers are made from the eligible list in the order the names appear on it. You will be notified of your grade and your rank as soon as all these computations have been made. This will be done as rapidly as possible.

People who are found to meet the requirements in the announcement are called "eligibles." Their names are put on a list of eligible candidates. An eligible's chances of getting a job depend on how high he stands on this list and how fast agencies are filling jobs from the list.

When a job is to be filled from a list of eligibles, the agency asks for the names of people on the list of eligibles for that job. When the civil service commission receives this request, it sends to the agency the names of the three people highest on this list. Or, if the job to be filled has specialized requirements, the office sends the agency the names of the top three persons who meet these requirements from the general list.

The appointing officer makes a choice from among the three people whose names were sent to him. If the selected person accepts the appointment, the names of the others are put back on the list to be considered for future openings.

That is the rule in hiring from all kinds of eligible lists, whether they are for typist, carpenter, chemist, or something else. For every vacancy, the appointing officer has his choice of any one of the top three eligibles on the list. This explains why the person whose name is on top of the list sometimes does not get an appointment when some of the persons lower on the list do. If the appointing officer chooses the second or third eligible, the No. 1 eligible does not get a job at once, but stays on the list until he is appointed or the list is terminated.

X. HOW TO PASS THE INTERVIEW TEST

The examination for which you applied requires an oral interview test. You have already taken the written test and you are now being called for the interview test – the final part of the formal examination.

You may think that it is not possible to prepare for an interview test and that there are no procedures to follow during an interview. Our purpose is to point out some things you can do in advance that will help you and some good rules to follow and pitfalls to avoid while you are being interviewed.

What is an interview supposed to test?

The written examination is designed to test the technical knowledge and competence of the candidate; the oral is designed to evaluate intangible qualities, not readily measured otherwise, and to establish a list showing the relative fitness of each candidate – as measured against his competitors – for the position sought. Scoring is not on the basis of "right" and "wrong," but on a sliding scale of values ranging from "not passable" to "outstanding." As a matter of fact, it is possible to achieve a relatively low score without a single "incorrect" answer because of evident weakness in the qualities being measured.

Occasionally, an examination may consist entirely of an oral test – either an individual or a group oral. In such cases, information is sought concerning the technical knowledges and abilities of the candidate, since there has been no written examination for this purpose. More commonly, however, an oral test is used to supplement a written examination.

Who conducts interviews?

The composition of oral boards varies among different jurisdictions. In nearly all, a representative of the personnel department serves as chairman. One of the members of the board may be a representative of the department in which the candidate would work. In some cases, "outside experts" are used, and, frequently, a businessman or some other representative of the general public is asked to serve. Labor and management or other special groups may be represented. The aim is to secure the services of experts in the appropriate field.

However the board is composed, it is a good idea (and not at all improper or unethical) to ascertain in advance of the interview who the members are and what groups they represent. When you are introduced to them, you will have some idea of their backgrounds and interests, and at least you will not stutter and stammer over their names.

What should be done before the interview?

While knowledge about the board members is useful and takes some of the surprise element out of the interview, there is other preparation which is more substantive. It *is* possible to prepare for an oral interview – in several ways:

1) Keep a copy of your application and review it carefully before the interview

This may be the only document before the oral board, and the starting point of the interview. Know what education and experience you have listed there, and the sequence and dates of all of it. Sometimes the board will ask you to review the highlights of your experience for them; you should not have to hem and haw doing it.

2) Study the class specification and the examination announcement

Usually, the oral board has one or both of these to guide them. The qualities, characteristics or knowledges required by the position sought are stated in these documents. They offer valuable clues as to the nature of the oral interview. For example, if the job involves supervisory responsibilities, the announcement will usually indicate that knowledge of modern supervisory methods and the qualifications of the candidate as a supervisor will be tested. If so, you can expect such questions, frequently in the form of a hypothetical situation which you are expected to solve. NEVER go into an oral without knowledge of the duties and responsibilities of the job you seek.

3) Think through each qualification required

Try to visualize the kind of questions you would ask if you were a board member. How well could you answer them? Try especially to appraise your own knowledge and background in each area, *measured against the job sought*, and identify any areas in which you are weak. Be critical and realistic – do not flatter yourself.

4) Do some general reading in areas in which you feel you may be weak

For example, if the job involves supervision and your past experience has NOT, some general reading in supervisory methods and practices, particularly in the field of human relations, might be useful. Do NOT study agency procedures or detailed manuals. The oral board will be testing your understanding and capacity, not your memory.

5) Get a good night's sleep and watch your general health and mental attitude

You will want a clear head at the interview. Take care of a cold or any other minor ailment, and of course, no hangovers.

What should be done on the day of the interview?

Now comes the day of the interview itself. Give yourself plenty of time to get there. Plan to arrive somewhat ahead of the scheduled time, particularly if your appointment is in the fore part of the day. If a previous candidate fails to appear, the board might be ready for you a bit early. By early afternoon an oral board is almost invariably behind schedule if there are many candidates, and you may have to wait. Take along a book or magazine to read, or your application to review, but leave any extraneous material in the waiting room when you go in for your interview. In any event, relax and compose yourself.

The matter of dress is important. The board is forming impressions about you – from your experience, your manners, your attitude, and your appearance. Give your personal appearance careful attention. Dress your best, but not your flashiest. Choose conservative, appropriate clothing, and be sure it is immaculate. This is a business interview, and your appearance should indicate that you regard it as such. Besides, being well groomed and properly dressed will help boost your confidence.

Sooner or later, someone will call your name and escort you into the interview room. *This is it.* From here on you are on your own. It is too late for any more preparation. But remember, you asked for this opportunity to prove your fitness, and you are here because your request was granted.

What happens when you go in?

The usual sequence of events will be as follows: The clerk (who is often the board stenographer) will introduce you to the chairman of the oral board, who will introduce you to the other members of the board. Acknowledge the introductions before you sit down. Do not be surprised if you find a microphone facing you or a stenotypist sitting by. Oral interviews are usually recorded in the event of an appeal or other review.

Usually the chairman of the board will open the interview by reviewing the highlights of your education and work experience from your application – primarily for the benefit of the other members of the board, as well as to get the material into the record. Do not interrupt or comment unless there is an error or significant misinterpretation; if that is the case, do not hesitate. But do not quibble about insignificant matters. Also, he will usually ask you some question about your education, experience or your present job – partly to get you to start talking and to establish the interviewing "rapport." He may start the actual questioning, or turn it over to one of the other members. Frequently, each member undertakes the questioning on a particular area, one in which he is perhaps most competent, so you can expect each member to participate in the examination. Because time is limited, you may also expect some rather abrupt switches in the direction the questioning takes, so do not be upset by it. Normally, a board member will not pursue a single line of questioning unless he discovers a particular strength or weakness.

After each member has participated, the chairman will usually ask whether any member has any further questions, then will ask you if you have anything you wish to add. Unless you are expecting this question, it may floor you. Worse, it may start you off on an extended, extemporaneous speech. The board is not usually seeking more information. The question is principally to offer you a last opportunity to present further qualifications or to indicate that you have nothing to add. So, if you feel that a significant qualification or characteristic has been overlooked, it is proper to point it out in a sentence or so. Do not compliment the board on the thoroughness of their examination – they have been sketchy, and you know it. If you wish, merely say, "No thank you, I have nothing further to add." This is a point where you can "talk yourself out" of a good impression or fail to present an important bit of information. Remember, *you close the interview yourself.*

The chairman will then say, "That is all, Mr. ______, thank you." Do not be startled; the interview is over, and quicker than you think. Thank him, gather your belongings and take your leave. Save your sigh of relief for the other side of the door.

How to put your best foot forward

Throughout this entire process, you may feel that the board individually and collectively is trying to pierce your defenses, seek out your hidden weaknesses and embarrass and confuse you. Actually, this is not true. They are obliged to make an appraisal of your qualifications for the job you are seeking, and they want to see you in your best light. Remember, they must interview all candidates and a non-cooperative candidate may become a failure in spite of their best efforts to bring out his qualifications. Here are 15 suggestions that will help you:

1) Be natural – Keep your attitude confident, not cocky

If you are not confident that you can do the job, do not expect the board to be. Do not apologize for your weaknesses, try to bring out your strong points. The board is interested in a positive, not negative, presentation. Cockiness will antagonize any board member and make him wonder if you are covering up a weakness by a false show of strength.

2) Get comfortable, but don't lounge or sprawl

Sit erectly but not stiffly. A careless posture may lead the board to conclude that you are careless in other things, or at least that you are not impressed by the importance of the occasion. Either conclusion is natural, even if incorrect. Do not fuss with your clothing, a pencil or an ashtray. Your hands may occasionally be useful to emphasize a point; do not let them become a point of distraction.

3) Do not wisecrack or make small talk

This is a serious situation, and your attitude should show that you consider it as such. Further, the time of the board is limited – they do not want to waste it, and neither should you.

4) Do not exaggerate your experience or abilities

In the first place, from information in the application or other interviews and sources, the board may know more about you than you think. Secondly, you probably will not get away with it. An experienced board is rather adept at spotting such a situation, so do not take the chance.

5) If you know a board member, do not make a point of it, yet do not hide it

Certainly you are not fooling him, and probably not the other members of the board. Do not try to take advantage of your acquaintanceship – it will probably do you little good.

6) Do not dominate the interview

Let the board do that. They will give you the clues – do not assume that you have to do all the talking. Realize that the board has a number of questions to ask you, and do not try to take up all the interview time by showing off your extensive knowledge of the answer to the first one.

7) Be attentive

You only have 20 minutes or so, and you should keep your attention at its sharpest throughout. When a member is addressing a problem or question to you, give him your undivided attention. Address your reply principally to him, but do not exclude the other board members.

8) Do not interrupt

A board member may be stating a problem for you to analyze. He will ask you a question when the time comes. Let him state the problem, and wait for the question.

9) Make sure you understand the question

Do not try to answer until you are sure what the question is. If it is not clear, restate it in your own words or ask the board member to clarify it for you. However, do not haggle about minor elements.

10) Reply promptly but not hastily

A common entry on oral board rating sheets is "candidate responded readily," or "candidate hesitated in replies." Respond as promptly and quickly as you can, but do not jump to a hasty, ill-considered answer.

11) Do not be peremptory in your answers

A brief answer is proper – but do not fire your answer back. That is a losing game from your point of view. The board member can probably ask questions much faster than you can answer them.

12) Do not try to create the answer you think the board member wants

He is interested in what kind of mind you have and how it works – not in playing games. Furthermore, he can usually spot this practice and will actually grade you down on it.

13) Do not switch sides in your reply merely to agree with a board member

Frequently, a member will take a contrary position merely to draw you out and to see if you are willing and able to defend your point of view. Do not start a debate, yet do not surrender a good position. If a position is worth taking, it is worth defending.

14) Do not be afraid to admit an error in judgment if you are shown to be wrong

The board knows that you are forced to reply without any opportunity for careful consideration. Your answer may be demonstrably wrong. If so, admit it and get on with the interview.

15) Do not dwell at length on your present job

The opening question may relate to your present assignment. Answer the question but do not go into an extended discussion. You are being examined for a *new* job, not your present one. As a matter of fact, try to phrase ALL your answers in terms of the job for which you are being examined.

Basis of Rating

Probably you will forget most of these "do's" and "don'ts" when you walk into the oral interview room. Even remembering them all will not ensure you a passing grade. Perhaps you did not have the qualifications in the first place. But remembering them will help you to put your best foot forward, without treading on the toes of the board members.

Rumor and popular opinion to the contrary notwithstanding, an oral board wants you to make the best appearance possible. They know you are under pressure – but they also want to see how you respond to it as a guide to what your reaction would be under the pressures of the job you seek. They will be influenced by the degree of poise you display, the personal traits you show and the manner in which you respond.

ABOUT THIS BOOK

This book contains tests divided into Examination Sections. Go through each test, answering every question in the margin. We have also attached a sample answer sheet at the back of the book that can be removed and used. At the end of each test look at the answer key and check your answers. On the ones you got wrong, look at the right answer choice and learn. Do not fill in the answers first. Do not memorize the questions and answers, but understand the answer and principles involved. On your test, the questions will likely be different from the samples. Questions are changed and new ones added. If you understand these past questions you should have success with any changes that arise. Tests may consist of several types of questions. We have additional books on each subject should more study be advisable or necessary for you. Finally, the more you study, the better prepared you will be. This book is intended to be the last thing you study before you walk into the examination room. Prior study of relevant texts is also recommended. NLC publishes some of these in our Fundamental Series. Knowledge and good sense are important factors in passing your exam. Good luck also helps. So now study this Passbook, absorb the material contained within and take that knowledge into the examination. Then do your best to pass that exam.

EXAMINATION SECTION

EXAMINATION SECTION

TEST 1

DIRECTIONS: Each question or incomplete statement is followed by several suggested answers or completions. Select the one that BEST answers the question or completes the statement. *PRINT THE LETTER OF THE CORRECT ANSWER IN THE SPACE AT THE RIGHT.*

1. It is often desirable for an administrator to consult, during the planning process, the persons to be affected by those plans. 1.____
Of the following, the MAJOR justification for such consultation is that it recognizes the
   A. fact that participating in horizontal planning is almost always more effective than participating in vertical planning
   B. principle of participation and the need for a sense of belonging as a means of decreasing resistance and developing support
   C. principle that lower-level administrators normally are more likely than higher-level administrators to emphasize longer-range goals
   D. fact that final responsibility for the approval of plans should be placed in committees not individuals

2. In evaluating performance and, if necessary, correcting what is being done to assure attainment of results according to plan, it is GENERALLY best for the administrator to do which one of the following? 2.____
   A. Make a continual effort to increase the number of written control reports prepared
   B. Thoroughly investigate in equal detail all possible deviations indicated by comparison of performance to expectation
   C. Decentralize, within an operating unit or division, the responsibility for correcting deviations
   D. Concentrate on the exceptions, or outstanding variations, from the expected results or standards

3. Generally, changes in the ways in which the supervisors and employees in an organization do things are MORE likely to be welcomed by them when the changes 3.____
   A. threaten the security of the supervisors than when they do not
   B. are inaugurated after prior change has been assimilated than when they are inaugurated before other major changes have been assimilated
   C. follow a series of failures in changes when they follow a series of successful changes
   D. are dictated by personal order rather than when they result from an application of previously established impersonal principles

4. For sound organization relationships, of the following, it is generally MOST desirable that 4.____
   A. authority and responsibility be segregated from each other, in order to facilitate control
   B. the authority of a manager should be commensurate with his responsibility, and vice versa
   C. authority be defined as the obligation of an individual to carry out assigned activities to the best of his or her ability
   D. clear recognition be given to the fact that delegation of authority benefits only the manager who delegates it

5. In utilizing a checklist of questions for general managerial planning, which one of the following generally is the FIRST question to be asked and answered? 5.____
   A. Where will it take place?
   B. How will it be done?
   C. Why must it be done?
   D. Who will do it?

6. Of the following, it is USUALLY best to set administrative objectives so that they are 6.____
   A. at a level that is unattainable, so that administrators will continually be strongly motivated
   B. at a level that is attainable, but requires some stretching and reaching by administrators trying to attain them
   C. stated in qualitative rather than quantitative terms whenever a choice between the two is possible
   D. stated in a general and unstructured manner, to permit each administrator maximum freedom in interpreting them

7. In selecting from among administrative alternatives, three general bases for decisions are open to the manager – experience, experimentation, and research and analysis. Of the following, the best argument AGAINST primary reliance upon experimentation as the method of evaluating administrative alternatives is that experimentation is 7.____
   A. generally the most expensive of the three techniques
   B. almost always legally prohibited in procedural matters
   C. possible only in areas where results may be easily duplicated by other experimenters at any time
   D. an approach that requires information on scientific method seldom available to administrators

8. The administrator who utilizes the techniques of operations research, linear programming and simulation in making an administrative decision should MOST appropriately be considered to be using the techniques of ______ analysis. 8.____
   A. intuitive B. quantitative
   C. nonmathematical D. qualitative

9. When an additional organizational level is added within a department, that department has MOST directly manifested 9.____
   A. horizontal growth B. horizontal shrinkage
   C. vertical growth D. vertical shrinkage

10. Of the following, the one which GENERALLY is the most intangible planning factor is 10.____
    A. budget dollars allocated to a function
    B. square feet of space for office use
    C. number of personnel in various clerical titles
    D. emotional impact of a proposed personnel policy among employees

11. Departmentation by function is the same as, or most similar to, departmentation by 11.____
    A. equipment B. clientele
    C. territory D. activity

12. Such verifiable factors as turnover, absenteeism or volume of grievances would generally BEST assist in measuring the effectiveness of a program to improve 12.____
    A. forms control B. employee morale
    C. linear programming D. executive creativity

13. An organization increases the number of subordinates reporting to a manager up to the point where incremental savings in costs, better communication and morale, and other factors equal incremental losses in effectiveness of control, direction and similar factors. This action MOST specifically employs the technique of 13.____
    A. role playing
    B. queuing theory
    C. marginal analysis
    D. capital standards analysis

14. The term *computer hardware* is MOST likely to refer to 14.____
    A. machines and equipment
    B. Ethernet and USB cables
    C. training manuals
    D. word processing and spreadsheet programs

15. Determining what is being accomplished, that is, evaluating the performance and, if necessary, applying corrective measures so that performance takes place according to plans is MOST appropriately called management 15.____
    A. actuating B. planning
    C. controlling D. motivating

16. Of the following, the BEST overall technique for choosing from among several alternative public programs proposed to try to achieve the same broad objective generally is ______ analysis. 16.____
    A. random-sample
    B. input
    C. cost-effectiveness
    D. output

17. When the success of a plan in achieving specific program objectives is measured against that plan's costs, the measure obtained is most directly that of the plan's 17.____
    A. pervasiveness
    B. control potential
    C. primacy
    D. efficiency

18. Generally, the degree to which an organization's planning will be coordinated varies MOST directly with the degree to which 18.____
    A. the individuals charged with executing plans are better compensated than those charged with developing and evaluating plans
    B. the individuals charged with planning understand and agree to utilize consistent planning premises
    C. a large number of position classification titles have been established for those individuals charged with organizational planning functions
    D. subordinate unit objectives are allowed to control the overall objectives of the departments of which such subordinate units are a part

19. The responsibility for specific types of decisions generally is BEST delegated to 19.____
    A. the highest organizational level at which there is an individual possessing the ability, desire, impartiality and access to relevant information needed to make these decisions
    B. the lowest organizational level at which there is an individual possessing the ability, desire, impartiality and access to relevant information needed to make these decisions
    C. a group of executives, rather than a single executive, if these decisions deal with an emergency
    D. the organizational level midway between that which will have to carry out these decisions and that which will have to authorize the resources for their implementation

20. The process of managing by objectives is MOST likely to lead to a situation in which the 20.____
    A. goal accomplishment objectives of managers tend to have a longer timespan as one goes lower down the line in an organization
    B. establishment of quantitative goals for staff positions is generally easier than the establishment of quantitative goals for line positions
    C. development of objectives requires the manager to think of the way he will accomplish given results, and of the organization, personnel and resources that he will need
    D. superiors normally develop and finally approve detailed goals for subordinates without any prior consultation with either those subordinates or with the top-level executives responsible for the longer-run objectives of the organization

21. As used with respect to decision making, the application of scientific method to the study of alternatives in a problem situation, with a view to providing a quantitative basis for arriving at an optimum solution in terms of the goals sought is MOST appropriately called 21.____
    A. simple number departmentation
    B. geographic decentralization
    C. operations research
    D. trait rating

22. Assume that a bureau head proposes that final responsibility and authority for all planning within the bureau is to be delegated to one employee who is to be paid at the level of an assistant division head in that bureau. 22.____
Of the following, the MOST appropriate comment about this proposal is that it's
    A. *improper*, mainly because planning does not call for someone at such a high level
    B. *improper*, mainly because responsibility for a basic management function such as planning may not properly be delegated as proposed
    C. *proper*, mainly because ultimate responsibility for all bureau planning is best placed as proposed
    D. *proper*, mainly because every well-managed bureau should have a full-time planning officer

23. Of the following, the MOST important reason that participation has motivating effects is generally that it gives to the individual participating 23.____
    A. a recognition of his or her desire to feel important and to contribute to achievement of worthwhile goals
    B. an opportunity to participate in work that is beyond the scope of the class specification for his or her title
    C. a secure knowledge that his or her organization's top leadership is as efficient as possible considering all major circumstances
    D. the additional information likely to be crucial to his or her promotion

24. Of the following, the MOST essential characteristic of an effective employee suggestion system is that 24.____
    A. suggestions be submitted upward through the chain of command
    B. suggestions be acted upon promptly so that employees may be promptly informed of what happens to their submitted suggestions
    C. suggesters be required to sign their names on the material sent to the actual evaluators for evaluation
    D. suggesters receive at least 25% of the agency's savings during the first two years after their suggestions have been accepted and put into effect by the agency

25. Two organizations have the same basic objectives and the same total number of employees. The span of authority of each intermediate manager is narrower in one organization than it is in the other. It is MOST likely that the organization in which each intermediate manager has a narrower span of authority will have 25.____
    A. fewer intermediate managers
    B. more organizational levels
    C. more managers reporting to a larger number of intermediate supervisors
    D. more characteristics of a *flat* organizational structure

KEY (CORRECT ANSWERS)

1. B
2. D
3. B
4. B
5. C

6. B
7. A
8. B
9. C
10. D

11. D
12. B
13. C
14. A
15. C

16. C
17. D
18. B
19. B
20. C

21. C
22. B
23. A
24. B
25. B

TEST 2

DIRECTIONS: Each question or incomplete statement is followed by several suggested answers or completions. Select the one that BEST answers the question or completes the statement. *PRINT THE LETTER OF THE CORRECT ANSWER IN THE SPACE AT THE RIGHT.*

1. Which one of the following BEST expresses the essence of the merit idea or system in public employment? 1.____
   A. A person's worth to the organization—the merit of his or her attributes and capacities—is the governing factor in his or her selection, assignment, pay, recognition, advancement and retention
   B. Written tests of the objective type are the only fair way to select on a merit basis from among candidates for open-competitive appointment to positions within the merit system
   C. Employees who have qualified for civil service positions shall have lifetime tenure during good behavior in those positions regardless of changes in public programs
   D. Periodic examinations with set date limits within which all persons desiring to demonstrate their merit may apply, shall be publicly advertised and held for all promotional titles

2. Of the following, the promotion selection policy generally considered MOST antithetical to the merit concept is the promotion selection policy which 2.____
   A. is based solely on objective tests of competence
   B. is based solely on seniority
   C. may require a manager to lose his or her best employee to another part of the organization
   D. permits operating managers collectively to play a significant role in promotion decisions

3. Of the following, the problems encountered by government establishments which are MOST likely to make extensive delegation of authority difficult to effectuate tend to be problems of 3.____
   A. accountability and ensuring uniform administration
   B. line and staff relationships within field offices
   C. generally employee opposition to such delegation of authority and to the subsequent record-keeping activities
   D. use of the management-by-objectives approach

4. The major decisions as to which jobs shall be created and who shall carry which responsibilities should GENERALLY be made by 4.____
   A. budgetary advisers
   B. line managers
   C. classification specialists
   D. peer-level rating committees

5. The ultimate controlling factor in structuring positions in the public service, MOST generally, should be the 5.____
   A. possibility of providing upgrading for highly productive employees
   B. collective bargaining demands initially made by established public employee unions
   C. positive motivational effects upon productivity resulting from an inverted pyramid job structure
   D. effectiveness of the structuring in serving the mission of the organization

6. Of the following, the most usual reason for unsatisfactory line-staff relationships is 6.____
   A. inept use of the abilities of staff personnel by line management
   B. the higher salaries paid to line officials
   C. excessive consultation between line officials and staff officials at the same organizational level
   D. a feeling among the staff members that only lower-level line members appreciate their work

7. Generally, an employee receiving new information from a fellow employee is MOST likely to 7.____
   A. forget the new information if it is consistent with his or her existing beliefs much more easily than he or she forgets the new information if it is inconsistent with existing beliefs
   B. accept the validity of the new information if it is consistent with his or her existing beliefs more readily than he or she accepts the validity of the new information if it is inconsistent with existing beliefs
   C. have a less accurate memory of the new information if it is consistent with his or her existing beliefs than he or she has of the new information if it is inconsistent with existing beliefs
   D. ignore the new information if it is consistent with his or her existing beliefs more often than he or she ignores the new information if it is inconsistent with existing beliefs

8. Virtually all of us use this principle in our human communications – perhaps without realizing it. In casual conversations, we are alert for cues to whether we are understood (e.g., attentive nods from the other person). Similarly, an instructor is always interested in reactions among those to whom he is giving instruction. The effective administrator is equally conscious of the need to determine his or her subordinates' reactions to what he or she is trying to communicate. 8.____
   The principle referred to in the above selection is MOST appropriately called
   A. cognitive dissonance B. feedback
   C. negative reinforcement D. noise transmission

9. Of the following, the PRINCIPAL function of an *ombudsman* generally is to 9.____
   A. review departmental requests for new data processing equipment so as to reduce duplication
   B. receive and investigate complaints from citizens who are displeased with the actions or non-actions of administrative officials and try to effectuate warranted remedies
   C. review proposed departmental reorganizations in order to advise the chief executive whether or not they are in accordance with the latest principles of proper management structuring
   D. presiding over courts of the judiciary convened to try *sitting* judges

10. Of the following, the MOST valid reason for recruiting an intermediate-level administrator from outside an agency, rather than from within the agency, normally is to 10.____
    A. improve the public image of the agency as a desirable place in which to be employed
    B. reduce the number of potential administrators who must be evaluated prior to filling the position
    C. minimize the morale problems arising from frequent internal staff upgradings
    D. obtain fresh ideas and a fresh viewpoint on agency problems

11. A MAJOR research finding regarding employee absenteeism is that 11.____
    A. absenteeism is likely to be higher on hot days
    B male employees tend to be absent more than female employees
    C. the way an employee is treated as a definite bearing on absenteeism
    D. the distance employees have to travel is one of the most important factors in absenteeism

12. Of the following, the supervisory behavior that is of GREATEST benefit to the organization is exhibited by supervisors who 12.____
    A. are strict with subordinates about following rules and regulations
    B. encourage subordinates to be interested in the work
    C. are willing to assist with subordinates' work on most occasions
    D. get the most done with available staff and resources

13. The management of time is one of the critical aspects of any supervisor's performance. 13.____
Therefore, in evaluating a subordinate from the viewpoint of how he manages time, a supervisor should rate HIGHEST the subordinate who
A. concentrates on each task as he undertakes it
B. performs at a standard and predictable pace under all circumstances
C. takes shortened lunch periods when he is busy
D. tries to do two things simultaneously

14. A MAJOR research finding regarding employee absenteeism is that 14.____
A. absenteeism is likely to be higher on hot days
B male employees tend to be absent more than female employees
C. the way an employee is treated as a definite bearing on absenteeism
D. the distance employees have to travel is one of the most important factors in absenteeism

15. Of the following, the supervisory behavior that is of GREATEST benefit to the organization is exhibited by supervisors who 15.____
A. are strict with subordinates about following rules and regulations
B. encourage subordinates to be interested in the work
C. are willing to assist with subordinates' work on most occasions
D. get the most done with available staff and resources

16. In order to maintain a proper relationship with a worker who is assigned to staff rather than line functions, a line supervisor should 16.____
A. accept all recommendations of the staff worker
B. include the staff worker in the conferences called by the supervisor for his subordinates
C. keep the staff worker informed of developments in the area of his staff assignment
D. require that the staff worker's recommendations be communicated to the supervisor through the supervisor's own superior

17. Of the following, the GREATEST disadvantage of placing a worker in a staff position under the direct supervision of the supervisor whom he advises is the possibility that the 17.____
A. staff worker will tend to be insubordinate because of a feeling of superiority over the supervisor
B. staff worker will tend to give advice of the type which the supervisor wants to hear or finds acceptable
C. supervisor will tend to be mistrustful of the advice of a worker of subordinate rank
D. supervisor will tend to derive little benefit from the advice because to supervise properly he should know at least as much as his subordinate

18. One factor which might be given consideration in deciding upon the optimum span of control of a supervisor over his immediate subordinates is the position of the supervisor in the hierarchy of the organization. 18.____
It is generally considered proper that the number of subordinates immediately supervised by a higher, upper echelon, supervisor
   A. is unrelated to and tends to form no pattern with the number of supervised by lower level supervisors
   B. should be about the same as the number supervised by a lower level supervisor
   C. should be larger than the number supervised by a lower level supervisor
   D. should be smaller than the number supervised by a lower level supervisor

19. Assume that you are a supervisor and have been assigned to assist the head of a large agency unit. He asks you to prepare a simple, functional organization chart of the unit. 19.____
Such a chart would be USEFUL for
   A. favorably impressing members of the public with the important nature of the agency's work
   B. graphically presenting staff relationships which may indicate previously unknown duplications, overlaps, and gaps in job duties
   C. motivating all employees toward better performance because they will have a better understanding of job procedures
   D. subtly and inoffensively making known to the staff in the unit that you are now in a position of responsibility

20. In some large organizations, management's traditional means of learning about employee dissatisfaction has been in the *open door policy*. 20.____
This policy USUALLY means that
   A. management lets it be known that a management representative is generally available to discuss employees' questions, suggestions, and complaints
   B. management sets up an informal employee organization to establish a democratic procedure for orderly representation of employees
   C. employees are encouraged to attempt to resolve dissatisfactions at the lowest possible level of authority
   D. employees are provided with an address or box so that they may safely and anonymously register complaints

KEY (CORRECT ANSWERS)

1.	B	11.	A
2.	A	12.	D
3.	D	13.	A
4.	B	14.	C
5.	A	15.	D
6.	A	16.	C
7.	B	17.	B
8.	B	18.	D
9.	D	19.	B
10.	C	20.	A

EXAMINATION SECTION

TEST 1

DIRECTIONS: Each question or incomplete statement is followed by several suggested answers or completions. Select the one that BEST answers the question or completes the statement. *PRINT THE LETTER OF THE CORRECT ANSWER IN THE SPACE AT THE RIGHT.*

1. In many instances, managers deliberately set up procedures and routines that more than one department or more than one employee is required to complete and verify an entire operation or transaction. 1.____
The MAIN reason for establishing such routines is generally to
   A. minimize the chances of gaps and deficiencies in feedback of information to management
   B. expand the individual employee's vision and concern for broader organizational objectives
   C. provide satisfaction of employees' social and egoistic needs through teamwork and horizontal communications
   D. facilitate internal control designed to prevent errors, whether intentional or accidental

2. Committees—sometimes referred to as boards, commissions, or task forces—are widely used in government to investigate certain problems or to manage certain agencies. 2.____
Of the following, the MOST serious limitation of the committee approach to management in government is that
   A. it reflects government's inability to delegate authority effectively to individual executives
   B. committee members do not usually have similar backgrounds, experience, and abilities
   C. it promotes horizontal communication at the expense of vertical communication
   D. the spreading out of responsibility to a committee often results in a willingness to settle for weak, compromise solutions

3. Of the following, the BEST reason for replacing methods of committees on a staggered or partial basis rather than replacing all members simultaneously is that this practice 3.____
   A. gives representatives of different interest groups a chance to contribute their ideas
   B. encourages continuity of policy since retained members are familiar with previous actions
   C. prevents the interpersonal frictions from building up and hindering the work of the group
   D. improves the quality of the group's recommendations and decisions by stimulating development of new ideas

4. Assume that in considering a variety of actions to take to solve a given problem, a manager decides to take no action at all. 4.____
According to generally accepted management practice, such a decision would be
   A. *proper*, because under normal circumstances it is better to make no decision
   B. *improper*, because inaction would be rightly construed as shunning one's responsibilities
   C. *proper*, since this would be a decision which might produce more positive results than the other alternatives
   D. *improper*, since such a solution would delay corrective action and exacerbate the problem

5. Some writers in the field of management assume that when a newly promoted manager has been informed by his superior about the subordinates he is to direct and the extent of his authority, that is all that is necessary. 5.____
However, thereafter, this new manager should realize that, for practical purposes, his authority will be effective ONLY when
   A. he accepts full responsibility for the actions of his subordinates
   B. his subordinates are motivated to carry out their assignments
   C. it derives from acceptable personal attributes rather than from his official position
   D. he exercises it in an authoritarian manner

6. A newly appointed manager is assigned to assist the head of a small developing agency handling innovative programs. Although this manager is a diligent worker, he does not delegate authority to middle- and lower-echelon supervisors. 6.____
The MOST important reason why it would be desirable to change this attitude toward delegation is because otherwise
   A. he may have to assume more responsibility for the actions of his subordinates than is implied in the authority delegated to him
   B. his subordinates will tend to produce innovative solutions on their own
   C. the agency will become a decentralized type of organization in which he cannot maintain adequate controls
   D. he may not have time to perform other essential tasks

7. All types of organizations and all functions within them are to varying degrees affected today by the need to understand the application of computer systems to management practices. 7.____
The one of the following purposes for which such systems would be MOST useful is to
   A. lower the costs of problem-solving by utilizing data that is already in the agency's control system correlated with new data
   B. stabilize basic patterns of the organization into long-term structures and relationships
   C. give instant solutions to complex problems
   D. affect savings in labor costs for office tasks involving non-routine complex problems

8. Compared to individual decision-making, group decision-making is burdened with the DISADVANTAGE of 8.____
   A. making snap judgments
   B. pressure to examine all relevant elements of the problem
   C. greater motivation needed to implement the decision
   D. the need to clarify problems for the group participants

9. Assume that a manager in an agency, faced with a major administrative problem, has developed a number of alternative solutions to the problem. 9.____
   Which of the following would be MOST effective in helping the manager make the best decision?
   A. *Experience*, because a manager can distill from the past the fundamental reasons for success or failure since the future generally duplicates the past
   B. *Experimentation*, because it is the method used in scientific inquiry and can be tried out economically in limited areas
   C. *Research analysis*, because it is generally less costly than most other methods and involves the interrelationships among the more critical factors that bear upon the goal sought
   D. *Value forecasting*, because it assigns numerical significance to the values of alternative tangible and intangible choices and indicates the degree of risk involved in each choice

10. Management information systems operate more effectively for managers than mere data tabulating systems because information systems 10.____
   A. eliminate the need for managers to tell information processors what is required
   B. are used primarily for staff rather than line functions
   C. are less expensive to operate than manual methods of data collection
   D. present and utilize data in a meaningful form

11. Project-type organizations are in widespread use today because they offer a number of advantages. 11.____
   The MOST important purpose of the project organization is to
   A. secure a higher degree of coordination than could be obtained in a conventional line structure
   B. provide an orderly way of phrasing projects in and out of organizations
   C. expedite routine administrative processes
   D. allow for rapid assessment of the status of any given project and its effect on agency productivity

12. A manager adjusts his plans for future activity by reviewing information about the performance of his subordinates. 12.____
   This is an application of the process of
   A. human factor impact
   B. coordinated response
   C. feedback communication
   D. reaction control

13. From the viewpoint of the manager in an agency, the one of the following which is the MOST constructive function of a status system or a rank system based on employee performance is that the system 13.____
   A. makes possible effective communication, thereby lessening social distances between organizational levels
   B. is helpful to employees of lesser ability because it provides them with an incentive to exceed their capacities
   C. encourages the employees to attain or exceed the goals set for them by the organization
   D. diminishes friction in assignment and work relationships of personnel

14. Some managers ask employees who have been newly hired by their agency and then assigned to their divisions or units such questions as: *What are your personal goals? What do you expect from your job? Why do you want to work for this organization?* 14.____
For a manager to ask these questions is GENERALLY considered
   A. *inadvisable*; these questions should have been asked prior to hiring the employee
   B. *inadvisable*; the answers will arouse subjective prejudices in the manager before he sees what kind of work the employee can do
   C. *advisable*; this approach indicates to the employee that the manager is interested in him as an individual
   D. *advisable*; the manager can judge how much of a disparity exists between the employee's goals and the agency's goals

15. Assume that you have prepared a report to your superior recommending a reorganization of your staff to eliminate two levels of supervision. The total number of employees would remain the same, with the supervisors of the two eliminated levels taking on staff assignments. 15.____
In your report, which one of the following should NOT be listed as an expected result of such a reorganization?
   A. Fewer breakdowns and distortions in communications to staff
   B. Greater need for training
   C. Broader opportunities for development of employee skills
   D. Fewer employee errors due to exercise of closer supervision and control

16. *Administration* has often been criticized as being unproductive in the sense that it seems far removed from the end products of an organization. 16.____
According to modern management thought, this criticism, for the most part, is
   A. *invalid*, because administrators make it possible for subordinates to produce goods or services by directing coordination, and controlling their activities
   B. *valid*, because most subordinates usually do the work required to produce goods and services with only general direction from their immediate superiors
   C. *invalid*, because administrators must see to all of the details associated with the production of services
   D. *valid*, because administrators generally work behind the scenes and are mainly concerned with long-range planning

17. A manager must be able to evaluate the relative importance of his decisions and establish priorities for carrying them out. 17.____
Which one of the following factors bearing on the relative importance of making a decision would indicate to a manager that he can delegate that decision to a subordinate or give it low priority? The
   A. decision concerns a matter on which strict confidentiality must be maintained
   B. community impact of the decision is great
   C. decision can be easily changed
   D. decision commits the agency to heavy expenditure of funds

18. Suppose that you are responsible for reviewing and submitting to your superior the monthly reports from ten field auditors. Despite your repeated warnings to these auditors, most of them hand in their reports close to or after the deadline dates, so that you have no time to return them for revision and find yourself working overtime to make the necessary corrections yourself. The deadline dates for the auditors' reports and your report cannot be changed. 18.____
Of the following, the MOST probable cause for this continuing situation is that
   A. these auditors need retraining in the writing of this type of report
   B. possible disciplinary action as a result of the delay by the auditors has not been impressed upon them
   C. the auditors have had an opportunity to provide you with feedback to explain the reasons for the delays
   D. you, as the manager, have not used disciplinary measures of sufficient severity to change their behavior

19. Assume that an agency desiring to try out a *management-by-objectives* program has set down the guidelines listed below to implement this activity. 19.____
Which one of these guidelines is MOST likely to present obstacles to the success of this type of program?
   A. Specific work objectives should be determined by top management for employees at all levels.
   B. Objectives should be specific, attainable, and preferably measurable as to units, costs, ratios, time, etc.
   C. Standards of performance should be either qualitative or quantitative, preferably quantitative.
   D. There should be recognition and rewards for successful achievement or objectives.

20. Of the following, the MOST meaningful way to express productivity where employees work a standard number of hours each day is in terms of the relationship between man- 20.____
   A. hours expended and number of work-units needed to produce the final product
   B. days expended and goods and services produced
   C. days and energy expended
   D. days expended and number of workers

21. Agencies often develop productivity indices for many of their activities. 21.____
Of the following, the MOST important use for such indices is generally to
A. measure the agency's output against its own performance
B. improve quality standards while letting productivity remain unchanged
C. compare outputs of the agency with outputs in private industry
D. determine manpower requirements

22. The MOST outstanding characteristic of staff authority, such as that of a public relations officer in an agency, as compared with line authority, is generally accepted to be 22.____
A. reliance upon personal attributes
B. direct relationship to the primary objectives of the organization
C. absence of the right to direct or command
D. responsibility for attention to technical details

23. In the traditional organization structure, there are often more barriers to upward communication than to downward communication. 23.____
From the viewpoint of a manager whose goal is to overcome obstacles to communication, this situation should be
A. *accepted*; the downward system is the more important since it is highly directive, giving necessary orders, instructions, and procedures
B. *changed*; the upward system should receive more emphasis than the downward system, which represents stifling bureaucratic authority
C. *accepted*; it is generally conceded that upward systems supply enough feedback for control purposes necessary to the organization's survival
D. *changed*; research has generally verified the need for an increase in upward communications to supply more information about employees' ideas, attitudes, and performance

24. A principal difficulty in productivity measurement for local government services is in defining and measuring output, a problem familiar to managers. A measurement that merely looks good, but which may be against the public interest, is another serious problem. Managers should avoid encouraging employees to take actions that lead to such measurements. 24.____
In accordance with the foregoing statement, it would be MOST desirable for a manager to develop a productivity measure that
A. correlates the actual productivity measure with impact on benefit to the citizenry
B. does not allow for a mandated annual increase in productivity
C. firmly fixes priorities for resource allocations
D. uses numerical output, by itself, in productivity incentive plans

25. For a manager, the MOST significant finding of the Hawthorne studies and experiments is that an employee's productivity is affected MOST favorably when the 25.____
A. importance of tasks is emphasized and there is a logical arrangement of work functions

B. physical surroundings and work conditions are improved
C. organization has a good public relations program
D. employee is given recognition and allowed to participate in decision-making

---

KEY (CORRECT ANSWERS)

1.	D	11.	A
2.	D	12.	C
3.	B	13.	C
4.	C	14.	A
5.	B	15.	D
6.	D	16.	A
7.	A	17.	C
8.	D	18.	D
9.	C	19.	A
10.	D	20.	B

21.	A
22.	C
23.	D
24.	A
25.	D

TEST 2

DIRECTIONS: Each question or incomplete statement is followed by several suggested answers or completions. Select the one that BEST answers the question or completes the statement. *PRINT THE LETTER OF THE CORRECT ANSWER IN THE SPACE AT THE RIGHT.*

1. Which one of the following is generally accepted by managers as the MOST difficult aspect of a training program in staff supervision? 1.____
   A. Determining training needs of the staff
   B. Evaluating the effectiveness of the courses
   C. Locating capable instructors to teach the courses
   D. Finding adequate space and scheduling acceptable times for all participants

2. Assume that, as a manager, you have decided to start a job enrichment program with the purpose of making jobs more varied and interesting in an effort to increase the motivation of a certain group of workers in your division. 2.____
   Which one of the following should generally NOT be part of this program?
   A. Increasing the accountability of these individuals for their own work
   B. Granting additional authority or job freedom to these employees in their job activities
   C. Mandating increased monthly production goals for this group of employees
   D. Giving each of these employees a complete unit of work

3. Both employer and employee have an important stake in effective preparation for retirement. 3.____
   According to modern management thinking, the one of the following which is probably the MOST important aspect of a sound pre-retirement program is to
   A. make assignments that utilize the employee's abilities fully
   B. reassign the employee to a less demanding position in the organization for the last year or two he is on the job
   C. provide the employee with financial data and other facts that would be pertinent to his retirement planning
   D. encourage the employee to develop interests and hobbies which are connected with the job

4. The civil service system generally emphasizes a policy of *promotion-from-within*. Employees in the direct line of promotion in a given occupational group are eligible for promotion to the next higher title in that occupational group. 4.____
   Which one of the following is LEAST likely to occur as a result of this policy and practice?
   A. Training time will be saved since employees in higher-level positions are already familiar with many agency rules, regulations, and procedures.
   B. The recruitment section will be able to show prospective employees that there are distinct promotional opportunities.

C. Employees will be provided with a clear-cut picture as to their possible career ladder.
D. Employees will be encouraged to seek broad-based training and education to enhance their promotability.

5. From a management point of view, the MAIAN drawback of seniority as opposed to merit as a basis for granting pay increases to workers is that a pay increase system based on seniority 5.____
A. is favored by unions
B. upsets organizational status relationships
C. may encourage mediocre performance by employees
D. is more difficult to administer than a merit plan

6. One of the actions that is often taken against employees in the non-uniformed forces who are accused of misconduct on the job is suspension without pay. The MOST justifiable reason for taking such action is to 6.____
A. ease an employee out of the agency
B. enable an investigation to be conducted into the circumstances of the offense
C. improve the performance of the employee when he returns to the job
D. punish the employee by imposing a hardship on him

7. A manager has had difficulty in getting good clerical employees to staff a filing section under his supervision. To add to his problems, one of his most competent senior clerks requests a transfer to the accounting division so that he can utilize his new accounting skill, which he is acquiring by going to college at night. The manager attempts to keep the senior clerk in his filing section by calling the director of personnel and getting him to promise not to authorize any transfer. 7.____
GENERALLY, this manager's action is
A. *desirable*; he should not help his staff to develop themselves if it means losing good people
B. *undesirable*; he should recommend that the senior clerk get a raise in the hope of preventing him from transferring to another section
C. *desirable*; it shows that the manager is concerned about the senior clerk's future performance
D. *undesirable*; it is good policy to transfer employees to the type of work they are interested in and for which they are acquiring training

8. One of your subordinates, a unit supervisor, comes to you, the division chief, because he feels that he is working out of title, and he suggests that his competitive class position should be reclassified to a higher title. 8.____
Which one of the following statements that the subordinate has made is generally LEAST likely to be a valid support for his suggestion?
A. The work he is doing conforms to the general statement of duties and responsibilities as described in the class specification for the next higher title in his occupational group.
B. Most of the typical tasks he performs are listed in the class specification for a title with a higher salary range and are not listed for his current title.

C. His education and experience qualifications far exceed the minimum requirements for the position he holds.
D. His duties and responsibilities have changed recently and are now similar to those of his supervisor.

9. Assume that a class specification for a competitive title used exclusively by your agency is outdated, and that no examination for the title has been given since the specification was issued. 9.____
Of the following, the MOST appropriate action for your agency to take is to
A. make the necessary changes and submit the revised class specification to the city civil service commission
B. write the personnel director to recommend that the class specification be updated, giving the reasons and suggested revisions
C. prepare a revised class specification and submit it to the office of management and budget for their approval
D. secure approval of the state civil service commission to update the class specification, and then submit the revised specification to the city civil service commission

10. Assume that an appropriate eligible list has been established and certified to your agency for a title in which a large number of provisionals are serving in your agency. 10.____
In order to obtain permission from the personnel director to retain some of them beyond the usual time limit set by rules (two months) following certification of the list, which one of the following conditions MUST apply?
A. The positions are sensitive and require investigation of eligibles prior to appointment.
B. Replacement of all provisionals within two months would impair essential public service.
C. Employees are required to work rotating shifts, including nights and weekends.
D. The duties of the positions require unusual physical effort and endurance.

11. Under the federally-funded Comprehensive Employment and Training Act (CETA), the hiring by the city of non-civil servants for CETA jobs is PROHIBITED when the 11.____
A. applicants are unemployed because of seasonal lay-offs in private industry
B. applicants do not meet U.S. citizenship and city residence requirements
C. jobs have minimum requirements of specialized professional or technical training and experience
D. jobs are comparable to those performed by laid-off civil servants

12. Assume you are in charge of the duplicating service in your agency. Since employees assigned to this operation lack a sense of accomplishment because the work is highly specialized and repetitive, your superior proposes to enlarge the jobs of these workers and asks you about your reaction to this strategy. 12.____

The MOST appropriate response for you to make is that job enlargement would be

A. *undesirable*, primarily because it would increase production costs
B. *undesirable*, primarily because it would diminish the quality of the output
C. *desirable*, primarily because it might make it possible to add an entire level of management to the organizational structure of your agency
D. *desirable*, primarily because it might make it possible to decrease the amount of supervision the workers will require

13. According to civil service law, layoff or demotion must be made in inverse order of seniority among employees permanently serving in the same title and layoff unit. 13.____
Which one of the following is now the CORRECT formula for computing seniority?
Total continuous service in the
A. competitive class only
B. competitive, non-competitive, or labor class
C. classified or unclassified services
D. competitive, non-competitive, exempt, and labor classes

14. Under which of the following conditions would an appointing officer be permitted to consider the sex of a candidate in making an employment decision? 14.____
When
A. the duties of the position require considerable physical effort or strength
B. the duties of the position are considered inherently dangerous
C. separate toilet facilities and dressing rooms for the sexes are unavailable and/or cannot be provided in any event
D. the public has indicated a preference to be served by persons of a specified sex

15. Assume that an accountant under your supervision signs out to the field to make an agency audit. It is later discovered that, although he had reported himself at work until 5 P.M. that day, he had actually left for home at 3:30 P.M. Although this accountant has worked for the city for ten years and has had an excellent performance record, he is demoted to a lower title in punishment for this breach of duty. 15.____
According to generally accepted thinking on personnel management, the disciplinary action taken in this case should be considered
A. *appropriate*; a lesser penalty might encourage repetition of the offense
B. *inappropriate*; the correct penalty for such a breach of duty should be dismissal
C. *appropriate*; the accountant's abilities may be utilized better in the new assignment
D. *inappropriate*; the impact of a continuing stigma and loss of salary is not commensurate with the offense committed

16. Line managers often request more funds for their units than are actually required to attain their current objectives. 16.____
Which one of the following is the MOST important reason for such inflated budget requests?
The
A. expectation that budget examiners will exercise their prerogative of budget cutting
B. line manager's interest in improving the performance of his unit is thereby indicated to top management
C. expectation that such requests will make it easier to obtain additional funds in future years
D. opinion that it makes sense to obtain additional funds and decide later how to use them

17. Integrating budgeting with program planning and evaluation in a city agency is GENERALLY considered to be 17.____
A. *undesirable*; budgeting must focus on the fiscal year at hand, whereas planning must concern itself with developments over a period of years
B. *desirable*; budgeting facilitates the choice-making process by evaluating the financial implications of agency programs and forcing cost comparisons among them
C. *undesirable*; accountants and statisticians with the required budgetary skills have little familiarity with the substantive programs that the agency is conducting
D. *desirable*; such a partnership increases the budgetary skills of planners, thus promoting more effective use of public resources

18. An aspect of the managerial function, a budget is described BEST as a 18.____
A. set of qualitative management controls over productivity
B. tool based on historical accounting reports
C. type of management plan expressed in quantitative terms
D. precise estimate of future quantitative and qualitative contingencies

19. Which one of the following is generally accepted as the MAJOR immediate advantage of installing a system of program budgeting? 19.____
It
A. encourages managers to relate their decisions to the agency's long-range goals
B. is a replacement for the financial or fiscal budget
C. decreases the need for managers to make trade-offs in the decision-making process
D. helps to adjust budget figures to provide for unexpected developments

20. Of the following, the BEST means for assuring necessary responsiveness of a budgetary program to changing conditions is by 20.____
A. overestimating budgetary expenditures by 15% and assigning the excess to unforeseen problem areas
B. underestimating budgetary expenditures by at least 20% and setting aside a reserve account in the same amount

C. reviewing and revising the budget at regular intervals so that it retains its character as a current document
D. establishing *budget-by-exception* policies for each division in the agency

21. According to expert thought in the area of budgeting, participation in the preparation of a government agency's budget should GENERALLY involve 21.____
A. only top management
B. only lower levels of management
C. all levels of the organization
D. only a central budget office or bureau

22. Of the following, the MOST useful guide to analysis of budget estimates for the coming fiscal year is a comparison with 22.____
A. appropriations as amended for the current fiscal year
B. manpower requirements for the previous two years
C. initial appropriations for the current fiscal year
D. budget estimates for the preceding five years

23. A manager assigned to analyze the costs and benefits associated with a program which the agency head proposes to undertake may encounter certain factors which cannot be measured in dollar terms. 23.____
In such a case, the manager should GENERALLY
A. ignore the factors which cannot be quantified
B. evaluate the factors in accordance with their degree of importance to the overall agency goals
C. give the factors weight equal to the weight given to measurable costs and benefits
D. assume that non-measurable costs and benefits will balance out against one another

24. If city employees believe that they are receiving adverse treatment in terms of training and disciplinary actions because of their national origin, they may file charges of discrimination with the Federal government's 24.____
A. Human Rights Commission
B. Public Employee Relations Board
C. Equal Employment Opportunity Commission
D. United States Department of Commerce

25. Under existing employment statutes, the city is obligated, as an employer, to take *affirmative action* in certain instances. 25.____
This requirement has been imposed to ensure that
A. employees who are members of minority groups, or women, be given special opportunities for training and promotion even though they are not available to other employees
B. employees or applicants for employment are treated without regard to race, color, religion, sex, or national origin

C. proof exists to show that the city has acted with good intentions in any case where it has disregarded this requirement
D. men and women are treated alike except where State law provides special hour or working conditions for women

KEY (CORRECT ANSWERS)

1. B
2. C
3. C
4. D
5. C

6. B
7. D
8. C
9. B
10. B

11. D
12. D
13. D
14. C
15. D

16. A
17. B
18. C
19. A
20. D

21. C
22. A
23. B
24. C
25. B

EXAMINATION SECTION

TEST 1

DIRECTIONS: Each question or incomplete statement is followed by several suggested answers or completions. Select the one that BEST answers the question or completes the statement. *PRINT THE LETTER OF THE CORRECT ANSWER IN THE SPACE AT THE RIGHT.*

1. In almost every organization there is a nucleus of highly important functions commonly designated as *management*. 1.____
   Which of the following statements BEST characterizes *management*?
   A. Getting things done through others
   B. The highest level of intelligence in any organization
   C. The process whereby democratic and participative activities are maximized
   D. The *first among equals*

2. Strategies in problem-solving are important to anyone aspiring to advancement in the field of administration. 2.____
   Which of the following is BEST classified as the first step in the process of problem-solving?
   A. Collection and organization of data
   B. The formulation of a plan
   C. The definition of the problem
   D. The development of a method and methodology

3. One of the objectives of preparing a budget is to
   A. create optimistic goals which each department can attempt to meet
   B. create an overall company goals by combining the budgets of the various departments
   C. be able to compare planned expenditures against actual expenditures
   D. be able to identify accounting errors

4. The rise in demand for *systems* personnel in industrial and governmental organizations over the past five years has been extraordinary. 4.____
   In which of the following areas would a *systems* specialist assigned to an agency be LEAST likely to be of assistance?
   A. Developing, recommending, and establishing an effective cost and inventory system
   B. Development and maintenance of training manuals
   C. Reviewing existing work procedures and recommending improvements
   D. Development of aptitude tests for new employees

5. Management experts have come to the conclusion that the traditional forms of motivation used in industry and government, which emphasize authority over and economic rewards for the employee, are no longer appropriate. 5.____

To which of the following factors do such experts attribute the GREATEST importance in producing this change?

A. The desire of employees to satisfy material needs has become greater and more complex.
B. The desire for social satisfaction has become the most important aspect of the job for the average worker.
C. With greater standardization of work processes, there has been an increase in the willingness of workers to accept discipline.
D. In general, employee organizations have made it more difficult for management to fire an employee.

6. In preparing a budget, it is usually considered advisable to start the initial phases of preparation at the operational level of management. 6.____
Of the following, the justification that management experts usually advance as MOST reasonable for this practice is that operating managers, as a consequence of their involvement, will

A. develop a background in finance or accounting
B. have an understanding of the organizational structure
C. tend to feel responsible for carrying out budget activities
D. have the ability to see the overall financial picture

7. An administrative officer has been asked by his superior to write a concise, factual report with objective conclusions and recommendations based on facts assembled by other researchers. 7.____
Of the following factors, the administrative officer should give LEAST consideration to

A. the educational level of the person or persons for whom the report is being prepared
B. the use to be made of the report
C. the complexity of the problem
D. his own feelings about the importance of the problem

8. In an agency, upon which of the following is a supervisor's effectiveness MOST likely to depend? 8.____
The

A. degree to which a supervisor allows subordinates to participate in the decision-making process and the setting of objectives
B. degree to which a supervisor's style meets management's objectives and subordinates' needs
C. strength and forcefulness of the supervisor in pursuing his objectives
D. expertise and knowledge of the supervisor has about the specific work to be done

9. For authority to be effective, which of the following is the MOST basic requirement? 9.____
Authority must be

A. absolute B. formalized C. accepted D. delegated

10. Management no longer abhors the idea of employees taking daily work breaks, but prefers to schedule such breaks rather than to allot to each employee a standard amount of free time to be taken off during the day as he wishes. Which of the following BEST expresses the reason management theorists give for the practice of scheduling such breaks? 10.____
    A. Many jobs fall into natural work units which are scheduled, and the natural time to take a break is at the end of the unit
    B. Taking a scheduled break permits socialization and a feeling of accomplishment
    C. Managers have concluded that scheduling rest periods seems to reduce the incidence of unscheduled ones
    D. Many office workers who really need such breaks are hesitant about taking them unless they are scheduled

11. The computer represents one of the major developments of modern technology. It is widely used in both scientific and managerial activities because of its many advantages. Which of the following is NOT an advantage gained by management in the use of the computer? A computer 11.___
    A. provides the manager with a greatly enlarged memory so that he can easily be provided with data for decision making
    B. relieves the manager of basic decision-making responsibility, thereby giving him more time for directing and controlling
    C. performs routine, repetitive calculations with greater precision and reliability than employees
    D. provides a capacity for rapid simulations of alternative solutions to problem solving

12. A supervisor of a unit in a division is usually responsible for all of the following EXCEPT 12.____
    A. the conduct of subordinates in the achievement of division objectives
    B. maintaining quality standards in the unit
    C. the protection and care of materials and equipment in the unit
    D. performing the most detailed tasks in the unit himself

13. You have been assigned to teach a new employee the functions and procedures of your office. In your introductory talk, which of the following approaches is PREFERABLE? 13.____
    A. Advise the new employee of the employee benefits and services available to him, over and above his salary
    B. Discuss honestly the negative aspects of departmental procedures and indicate methods available to overcome them
    C. Give the new employee an understanding of the general purpose of office procedures and functions and of their relevance to departmental objectives
    D. Give a basic and detailed explanation of the operations of your office, covering all functions and procedures

14. It is your responsibility to assign work to several clerks under your supervision. One of the clerks indignantly refuses to accept an assignment and asks to be given something else. He has not yet indicated why he does not want the assignment, but is sitting there glaring at you, awaiting your reaction. 14.____
Of the following, which is the FIRST action you should take?
A. Ask the employee into your office in order to reprimand him and tell him emphatically that he must accept the assignment
B. Talk to the employee privately in an effort to find the reason for his indignation and refusal, and then base your action upon your findings
C. Let the matter drop for a day or two to allow the employee to cool off before you insist that he accept the assignment
D. Inform the employee quietly and calmly that as his supervisor you have selected him for this assignment and that you fully expect him to accept it

15. Administrative officers are expected to be able to handle duties delegated to them by their supervisors and to be able, as they advance in status, to delegate tasks to assistants. 15.____
When considering whether to delegate tasks to a subordinate, which of the following questions should be LEAST important to an administrative officer?
In the delegated tasks,
A. how significant are the decisions to be made, and how much consultation will be involved?
B. to what extent is uniformity and close coordination of activity required?
C. to what extent must speedy-on-the-spot decisions be made?
D. to what extent will delegation relieve the administrative officer of his burden of responsibility?

16. A functional forms file is a collection of forms which are grouped by 16.____
A. purpose B. department C. title D. subject

17. All of the following are reasons to consult a records retention schedule except one. 17.____
Which one is that?
To determine
A. whether something should be filed
B. how long something should stay in file
C. who should be assigned to filing
D. when something on file should be destroyed

18. Listed below are four of the steps in the process of preparing correspondence for filing. 18.____
If they were to be put in logical sequence, the SECOND step would be
A. preparing cross-reference sheets or cards
B. coding the correspondence using a classification system
C. sorting the correspondence in the order to be filed
D. checking for follow-up action required and preparing a follow-up slip

19. New material added to a file folder should USUALLY be inserted 19.____
    A. in the order of importance (the most important in front)
    B. in the order of importance (the most important in back)
    C. chronologically (most recent in front)
    D. chronologically (most recent in back)

20. An individual is looking for a name in the white pages of a telephone directory. Which of the following BEST describes the system of filing found there? 20.____
    A(n) _____ file
    A. alphabetic B. sequential C. locator D. index

21. The MAIN purpose of a tickler file is to 21.____
    A. help prevent overlooking matters that require future attention
    B. check on adequacy of past performance
    C. pinpoint responsibility for recurring daily tasks
    D. reduce the volume of material kept in general files

22. Which of the following BEST describes the process of reconciling a bank statement? 22.____
    A. Analyzing the nature of the expenditures made by the office during the preceding month
    B. Comparing the statement of the bank with the banking records maintained in the office
    C. Determining the liquidity position by reading the bank statement carefully
    D. Checking the service charges noted on the bank statement

23. From the viewpoint of preserving agency or institutional funds, which of the following is the LEAST acceptable method for making a payment? 23.____
    A check made out to
    A. cash B. a company
    C. an individual D. a partnership

24. In general, the CHIEF economy of using multicopy forms is in 24.____
    A. the paper on which the form is printed
    B. printing the form
    C. employee time
    D. carbon paper

25. Suppose your supervisor has asked you to develop a form to record certain information needed. 25.____
    The FIRST thing you should do is to
    A. determine the type of data that will be recorded repeatedly so that it can be preprinted
    B. study the relationship of the form to the job to be accomplished so that the form can be planned
    C. determine the information that will be recorded in the same place on each copy of the form so that it can be used as a check
    D. find out who will be responsible for supplying the information so that space can be provided for their signatures

26. An administrative officer in charge of a small fund for buying office supplies has just written a check to Charles Laird, a supplier, and has sent the check by messenger to him. A half-hour later, the messenger telephones the administrative officer. He has lost the check. 26.____
Which of the following is the MOST important action for the administrative officer to take under these circumstances?
   A. Ask the messenger to return and write a report describing the loss of the check
   B. Make a note on the performance record of the messenger who lost the check
   C. Take the necessary steps to have payment stopped on the check
   D. Refrain from doing anything since the check may be found shortly

27. A petty cash fund is set up PRIMARILY to 27.____
   A. take care of small investments that must be made from time to time
   B. take care of small expenses that arise from time to time
   C. provide a fund to be used as the office wants to use it with little need to maintain records
   D. take care of expenses that develop during emergencies, such as machine breakdowns and fires

28. Of the following, which is usually the MOST important guideline in writing business letters? 28.____
A letter should be
   A. neat
   B. written in a formalized style
   C. written in clear language intelligible to the reader
   D. written in the past tense

29. Suppose you are asked to edit a policy statement. You note that personal pronouns like *you*, *we*, and *I* are used freely. 29.____
Which of the following statements BEST applies to this use of personal pronouns?
It
   A. is proper usage because written business language should not be different from carefully spoken business language
   B. requires correction because is it ungrammatical
   C. is proper because it is clearer and has a warmer tone
   D. requires correction because policies should be expressed in an impersonal manner

30. Good business letters are coherent. 30.____
To be coherent means to
   A. keep only one unifying idea in the message
   B. present the total message
   C. use simple, direct words for the message
   D. tie together the various ideas in the message

31. Proper division of a letter into paragraphs requires that the writer of business letters should, as much as possible, be sure that 31.____
   A. each paragraph is short
   B. each paragraph develops discussion of just one topic
   C. each paragraph repeats the theme of the total message
   D. there are at least two paragraphs for every message

32. An editor is given a letter with this initial paragraph: 32.____
We have received your letter, which we read with interest, and we are happy to respond to your question. In fact, we talked with several people in our office to get ideas to send to you.
Which of the following is MOST reasonable for the editor to conclude?
The paragraph is
   A. concise
   B. communicating something of value
   C. unnecessary
   D. coherent

33. As soon as you pick up the phone, a very angry caller begins immediately to complain about city agencies and *red tape*. He says that he has been shifted to two or three different offices. It turns out that he is seeking information which is not immediately available to you. You believe you know, however, where it can be found. 33.____
Which of the following actions is the BEST one for you to take?
   A. To eliminate all confusion, suggest that the caller write the mayor stating explicitly what he wants
   B. Apologize by telling the caller how busy city agencies now are, but also tell him directly that you do not have the information he needs
   C. Ask for the caller's telephone number and assure him you will call back after you have checked further
   D. Give the caller the name and telephone number of the person who might be able to help, but explain that you are not positive he will get results

34. Suppose that one of your duties is to dictate responses to routine requests from the public for information. A letter writer asks for information which, as expressed in a one-sentence, explicit agency rule, cannot be given out to the public. 34.____
Of the following ways of answering the letter, which is the MOST efficient?
   A. Quote verbatim that section of the agency rules which prohibit giving this information to the public
   B. Without quoting the rule, explain why you cannot accede to the request and suggest alternative sources
   C. Describe how carefully the request was considered before classifying it as subject to the rule forbidding the issuance of such information
   D. Acknowledge receipt of the letter and advise that the requested information is not released to the public

35. Suppose you assist in supervising a staff which has rather high morale, and your own supervisor asks you to poll the staff to find out who will be able to work overtime this particular evening to help complete emergency work. 35.____
Which of the following approaches would be MOST likely to win their cooperation while maintaining their morale?
   A. Tell them that the better assignments will be given only to those who work overtime
   B. Tell them that occasional overtime is a job requirement
   C. Assure them they'll be doing you a personal favor
   D. Let them know clearly why the overtime is needed

36. Suppose that you have been asked to write and to prepare for reproduction new departmental vacation leave regulations. 36.____
After you have written the new regulations, all of which fit on one page, which one of the following would be the BESST method of reproducing 1,000 copies?
   A. An outside private printer, because you can best maintain confidentiality using this technique
   B. Xeroxing, because the copies will have the best possible appearance
   C. Typing copies, because you will be certain that there are the fewest possible errors
   D. Including it in the next company newsletter

37. Administration is the center, but not necessarily the source, of all ideas for procedural improvement. 37.____
The MOST significant implication that this principle bears for the administrative officer is that
   A. before procedural improvements are introduced, they should be approved by a majority of the staff
   B. it is the unique function of the administrative officer to derive and introduce procedural improvements
   C. the administrative officer should derive ideas and suggestions for procedural improvement from all possible sources, introducing any that promise to be effective
   D. the administrative officer should view employee grievances as the chief source of procedural improvements

38. Your bureau is assigned an important task. 38.____
Of the following, the function that you, as an administrative officer, can LEAST reasonably be expected to perform under these circumstances is
   A. division of the large job into individual tasks
   B. establishment of *production lines* within the bureau
   C. performance personally of a substantial share of all the work
   D. check up to see that the work has been done well

39. Suppose that you have broken a complex job into its smaller components before making assignments to the employees under your jurisdiction. 39.____
Of the following, the LEAST advisable procedure to follow from that point is to
   A. give each employee a picture of the importance of his work for the success of the total job
   B. establish a definite line of work flow and responsibility
   C. post a written memorandum of the best method for performing each job
   D. teach a number of alternative methods for doing each job

40. As an administrative officer, you are requested to draw up an organization chart of the whole department. 40.____
Of the following, the MOST important characteristic of such a chart is that it will
   A. include all peculiarities and details of the organization which distinguish it from any other
   B. be a schematic representation of purely administrative functions within the department
   C. present a modification of the actual departmental organization in the light of principles of scientific management
   D. present an accurate picture of the lines of authority and responsibility

KEY (CORRECT ANSWERS)

1.	A	11.	B	21.	A	31.	B
2.	C	12.	D	22.	B	32.	C
3.	C	13.	C	23.	A	33.	C
4.	D	14.	B	24.	C	34.	A
5.	D	15.	D	25.	B	35.	D
6.	C	16.	A	26.	C	36.	B
7.	D	17.	C	27.	B	37.	C
8.	B	18.	A	28.	C	38.	C
9.	C	19.	C	29.	D	39.	D
10.	C	20.	A	30.	D	40.	D

TEST 2

DIRECTIONS: Each question or incomplete statement is followed by several suggested answers or completions. Select the one that BEST answers the question or completes the statement. *PRINT THE LETTER OF THE CORRECT ANSWER IN THE SPACE AT THE RIGHT.*

Questions 1-10.

DIRECTIONS: In each of Questions 1 through 10, a pair of related words written in capital letters is followed by four other pairs of words. For each question, select the pair of words which MOST closely expresses a relationship similar to that of the pair in capital letters.

SAMPLE QUESTION:
BOAT – DOCK

A. air plane – hangar
B. rain – snow
C. cloth – cotton
D. hunger - food

Choice A is the answer to this sample question since, of the choices given, the relationship between airplane and hangar is most similar to the relationship between boat and dock.

1. AUTOMOBILE – FACTORY 1.____
   A. tea – lemon
   B. wheel – engine
   C. pot – flower
   D. paper – mill

2. GIRDER – BRIDGE 2.____
   A. petal – flower
   B. street – sidewalk
   C. meat – vegetable
   D. sun – storm

3. RADIUS – CIRCLE 3.____
   A. brick – building
   B. tie – tracks
   C. spoke – wheel
   D. axle – tire

4. DISEASE – RESEARCH 4.____
   A. death – poverty
   B. speech – audience
   C. problem – conference
   D. invalid – justice

5. CONCLUSION – INTRODUCTION 5.____
   A. commencement – beginning
   B. housing – motor
   C. caboose – engine
   D. train – cabin

6. SOCIETY – LAW 6.____
   A. baseball – rules
   B. jury – law
   C. cell – prisoner
   D. sentence – jury

7. PLAN – ACCOMPLISHMENT 7.____
   A. deed – fact B. method – success
   C. graph – chart D. rules – manual

8. ORDER – GOVERNMENT 8.____
   A. chaos – administration B. confusion – pandemonium
   C. rule – stability D. despair – hope

9. TYRANNY – FREEDOM 9.____
   A. despot – mob B. wealth – poverty
   C. nobility – commoners D. dictatorship – democracy

10. FAX – LETTER 10.____
   A. hare – tortoise B. lie – truth
   C. number – word D. report – research

Questions 11-16.

DIRECTIONS: Questions 11 through 16 are to be answered SOLELY on the basis of the information given in the passage below.

Inherent in all organized endeavors is the need to resolve the individual differences involved in conflict. Conflict may be either a positive or negative factor, since it may lead to creativity, innovation, and progress, on the one hand, or it may result, on the other hand, in a deterioration or even destruction of the organization. Thus, some forms of conflict are desirable, whereas others are undesirable and ethically wrong.

There are three management strategies which deal with interpersonal conflict. In the "divide-and-rule strategy," management attempts to maintain control by limiting the conflict to those directly involved and preventing their disagreement from spreading to the larger group. The "suppression –of-differences strategy" entails ignoring conflicts or pretending they are irrelevant. In the "working-through-differences strategy," management actively attempts to solve or resolve intergroup or interpersonal conflicts. Of the three strategies, only the last directly attacks and has the potential for eliminating the causes of conflict. An essential part of this strategy, however, is its employment by a committed and relatively mature management team.

11. According to the above passage, the *divide-and-rule strategy* for dealing with conflict is the attempt to 11.____
   A. involve other people in the conflict
   B. restrict the conflict to those participating in it
   C. divide the conflict into positive and negative factors
   D. divide the conflict into a number of smaller ones

12. The word *conflict* is used in relation to both positive and negative factors in this passage. 12.____
   Which one of the following words is MOST likely to describe the activity which the word *conflict*, in the sense of the passage, implies?
   A. Competition B. Cooperation C. Confusion D. Aggression

13. According to the above passage, which one of the following characteristics is shared by both the *suppression-of-difference strategy* and the *divide-and-rule strategy*? 13.____
    A. Pretending that conflicts are irrelevant
    B. Preventing conflicts from spreading to the group situation
    C. Failure to directly attack the causes of conflict
    D. Actively attempting to resolve interpersonal conflict

14. According to the above passage, the successful resolution of interpersonal conflict requires 14.____
    A. allowing the group to mediate conflicts between two individuals
    B. division of the conflict into positive and negative factors
    C. involvement of a committed, mature management team
    D. ignoring minor conflicts until they threaten the organization

15. Which can be MOST reasonably inferred from the above passage? A conflict between two individuals is LEAST likely to continue when management uses 15.____
    A. the *working-through-differences strategy*
    B. the *suppression-of-differences strategy*
    C. the *divide-and-rule strategy*
    D. a combination of all three strategies

16. According to the above passage, a DESIRABLE result of conflict in an organization is when conflict 16.____
    A. exposes production problems in the organization
    B. can be easily ignored by management
    C. results in advancement of more efficient managers
    D. leads to development of new methods

Questions 17-23.

DIRECTIONS: Questions 17 through 23 are to be answered SOLELY on the basis of the information given in the passage below.

Modern management places great emphasis on the concept of communication. The communication process consists of the steps through which an idea or concept passes from its inception by one person, the sender, until it is acted upon by another person, the receiver. Through an understanding of these steps and some of the possible barriers that may occur, more effective communication may be achieved. The first step in the communication process is ideation by the sender. This is the formation of the intended content of the message he wants to transmit. In the next step, encoding, the sender organizes his ideas into a series of symbols designed to communicate his message to his intended receiver. He selects suitable words or phrases that can be understood by the receiver, and he also selects the appropriate media to be used—for example, memorandum, conference, etc. The third step is transmission of the encoded message through selected channels in the organizational structure. In the fourth step, the receiver enters the process by tuning in to receive the message. If the receiver does not function, however, the message is lost. For example, if the message is oral, the receiver must be a good listener. The fifth step is decoding of the message by the receiver, as for example, by changing words into ideas. At this step, the decoded message may not be the same idea that the sender originally encoded because the sender and receiver have different perceptions regarding the meaning of certain words.

Finally, the receiver acts or responds. He may file the information, ask for more information, or take other action. There can be no assurance, however, that communication has taken place unless there is some type of feedback to the sender in the form of an acknowledgement that the message was received.

17. According to the above passage, *ideation* is the process by which the 17.____
    A. sender develops the intended content of the message
    B. sender organizes his ideas into a series of symbols
    C. receiver tunes in to receive the message
    D. receiver decodes the message

18. In the last sentence of the passage, the word *feedback* refers to the process by which the sender is assured that the 18.____
    A. receiver filed the information
    B. receiver's perception is the same as his own
    C. message was received
    D. message was poorly interpreted

19. Which one of the following BEST shows the order of the steps in the communication process as described in the passage? 19.____
    A. 1 – ideation 2 – encoding
       3 – decoding 4 – transmission
       5 – receiving 6 – action
       7 – feedback to the sender
    B. 1 – ideation 2 – encoding
       3 – transmission 4 – decoding
       5 – receiving 6 – action
       7 – feedback to the sender
    C. 1 – ideation 2 – decoding
       3 – transmission 4 – receiving
       5 – encoding 6 – action
       7 – feedback to the sender
    D. 1 – ideation 2 – encoding
       3 – transmission 4 – receiving
       5 – decoding 6 – action
       7 – feedback to the sender

20. Which one of the following BEST expresses the main theme of the passage? 20.____
    A. Different individuals have the same perceptions regarding the meaning of words.
    B. An understanding of the steps in the communication process may achieve better communication.
    C. Receivers play a passive role in the communication process.
    D. Senders should not communicate with receivers who transmit feedback.

21. The above passage implies that a receiver does NOT function properly when he 21.____
    A. transmits feedback
    B. files the information
    C. is a poor listener
    D. asks for more information

22. Which of the following, according to the above passage, is included in the SECOND step of the communication process? 22.____
    A. Selecting the appropriate media to be used in transmission
    B. Formulation of the intended content of the message
    C. Using appropriate media to respond to the receiver's feedback
    D. Transmitting the message through selected channels in the organization

23. The above passage implies that the *decoding* process is MOST NEARLY the reverse of the _____ process. 23.____
    A. transmission
    B. receiving
    C. feedback
    D. encoding

Questions 24-27.

DIRECTIONS: Questions 24 through 27 are to be answered SOLELY on the basis of the information given in the passage below.

A personnel researcher has at his disposal various approaches for obtaining information, analyzing it, and arriving at conclusions that have value in predicting and affecting the behavior of people at work. The type of method to be used depends on such factors as the nature of the research problem, the available data, and the attitude of those people being studied to the various kinds of approaches. While the experimental approach, with its use of control groups, is the most refined type of study, there are others that are often found useful in personnel research. Surveys, in which the researcher obtains facts on a problem from a variety of sources, are employed in research on wages, fringe benefits, and labor relations. Historical studies are used to trace the development of problems in order to understand them better and to isolate possible causative factors. Case studies are generally developed to explore all the details of a particular problem that is representative of other similar problems. A researcher chooses the most appropriate form of study for the problem he is investigating. He should recognize, however, that the experimental method, commonly referred to as the scientific method, if used validly and reliably, gives the most conclusive results.

24. The above statement discusses several approaches used to obtain information on particular problems. 24.____
    Which of the following may be MOST reasonably concluded from the passage? A(n)
    A. historical study cannot determine causative factors
    B. survey is often used in research on fringe benefits
    C. case study is usually used to explore a problem that is unique and unrelated to other problems
    D. experimental study is used when the scientific approach to a problem fails

25. According to the above passage, all of the following are factors that may determine the type of approach a researcher uses EXCEPT 25.____
   A. the attitudes of people toward being used in control groups
   B. the number of available sources
   C. his desire to isolate possible causative factors
   D. the degree of accuracy he requires

26. The words *scientific method*, used in the last sentence of the paragraph, refer to a type of study which, according to the paragraph, 26.____
   A. uses a variety of sources
   B. traces the development of problems
   C. uses control group
   D. analyzes the details of a representative problem

27. Which of the following can be MOST reasonably concluded from the above passage? 27.____
   In obtaining and analyzing information on a particular problem, a researcher employs the method which is the
   A. most accurate
   B. most suitable
   C. least expensive
   D. least time-consuming

Questions 28-31.

DIRECTIONS: Questions 28 through 31 are to be answered according to the information given in the following graph, which indicates at 5-year intervals the number of citations issued for various offenses from the year 2000 to the year 2020.

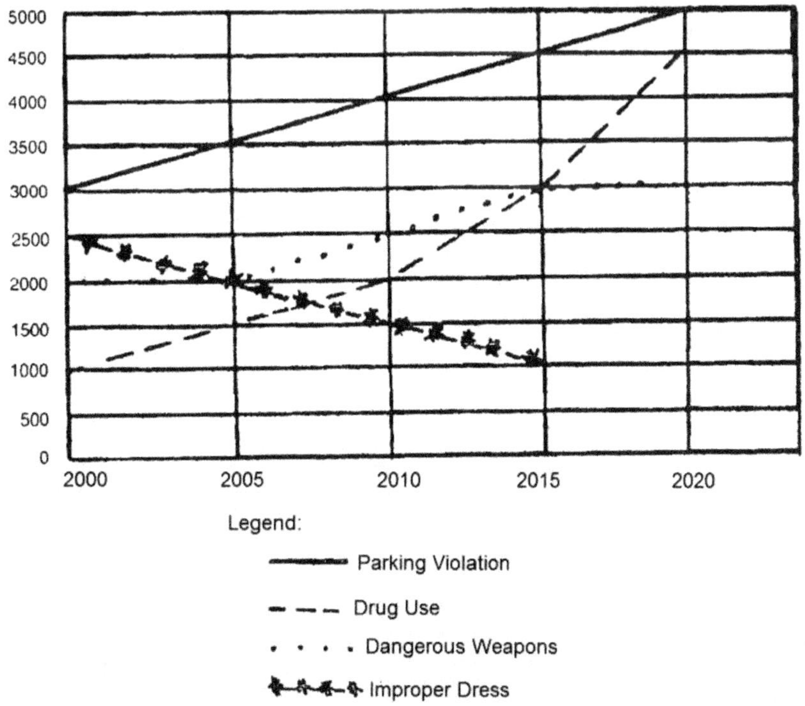

28. Over the 20-year period, which offense shows an AVERAGE rate of increase of more than 150 citations per year? 28.____
   A. Parking Violations
   B. Dangerous Weapons
   C. Drug Use
   D. None of the above

29. Over the 20-year period, which offense shows a CONSTANT rate of increase or decrease? 29.____
   A. Parking Violations
   B. Drug Use
   C. Dangerous Weapons
   D. Improper Dress

30. Which offense shows a TOTAL INCREASE OR DECREASE of 50% for the full 20-year period? 30.____
   A. Parking Violations
   B. Drug Use
   C. Dangerous Weapons
   D. Improper Dress

31. The percentage increase in total citations issued from 2005 to 2010 is MOST NEARLY 31.____
   A. 7%
   B. 11%
   C. 21%
   D. 41%

Questions 32-35.

DIRECTIONS: Questions 32 through 35 are to be answered SOLELY on the basis of the information given in the following chart, which shows the annual number of administrative actions completed for the four divisions of a bureau. Assume that the figures remain stable from year to year.

	DIVISIONS				
Administrative Actions	W	X	Y	Z	TOTALS
Telephone Inquiries Answered	8,000	6,800	7,500	4,800	27,100
Interviews Conducted	500	630	550	500	2,180
Applications Processed	15,000	18,000	14,500	9,500	57,000
Letters Typed	2,500	4,400	4,350	3,250	14,500
Reports Completed	200	250	100	50	600
Totals	26,200	30,080	27,000	18,100	101,380

32. In which division is the number of Applications Processed the GREATEST percentage of the total Administrative Action for that division? 32.____
   A. W
   B. X
   C. Y
   D. Z

33. The bureau chief is considering a plant that would consolidate the typing of letters in a separate unit. This unit would be responsible for the typing of letters for all divisions in which the number of letters typed exceeds 15% of the total number of Administrative Actions. 33.____
   Under this plan, which of the following divisions would CONTINUE to type its own letters?
   A. W and X
   B. W, X, and Y
   C. X and Y
   D. X and Z

34. The setting up of a central information service that would be capable of answering 25% of the whole bureau's telephone inquiries is under consideration. Under such a plan, the divisions would gain for other activities that time previously spent on telephone inquiries. 34.____
Approximately how much total time would such a service gain for all four divisions if it requires 5 minutes to answer the average telephone inquiry?
_____ hours.
A. 500 B. 515 C. 565 D. 585

35. Assume that the rate of production shown in the table can be projected as accurate for the coming year and that monthly output is constant for each type of administrative action within a division. Division Y is scheduled to work exclusively on a 4-month long special project during that year. During the period of the project, Division Y's regular workload will be divided evenly among the remaining divisions. 35.____
Using the figures in the table, what would be MOST NEARLY the percentage increase in the total Administrative Actions completed by Division Z for the year?
A. 8% B. 16% C. 25% D. 50%

36. You have conducted a traffic survey a 10 two-lane bridges and find the traffic between 4:30 and 5:30 P.M. average 665 cars per bridge that hour. You can't find the tabulation sheet for Bridge #7, but you know that 6066 cars were counted at the other 9 bridges. 36.____
Determine from this how many must have been counted at Bridge #7.
A. 584 B. 674 C. 665 D. 607

37. You pay temporary help $11.20 per hour and regular employees $12.00 per hour. Your workload is temporarily heavy, so you need 20 hours of extra regular employees' time to catch up. If you do this on overtime, you must pay time-and-a-half. If you use temporary help, it takes 25% more time to do the job. 37.____
What is the difference in cost between the two alternatives?
A. $20 more for temporary
B. $40 more for temporary
C. $80 more for regular
D. $136 more for regular

38. An experienced clerk can process the mailing of annual forms in 9 day. A new clerk takes 14 days to process them. 38.____
If they work together, how many days MOST NEARLY will it take to do the processing?
A. 4½ B. 5½ C. 6½ D. 7

39. A certain administrative aide is usually able to successfully handle 27% of all telephone inquiries without assistance. In a particular month, he receives 1,200 inquiries and handles 340 of them successfully on his own. 39.____
How many more inquiries has he handled successfully in that month than would have been expected of him based on his usual rate?
A. 10 B. 16 C. 24 D. 44

40. Suppose that on a scaled drawing of an office building floor, ½ inch represents three feet of actual floor dimensions. 40.____
A floor which is, in fact, 75 feet wide and 132 feet long has which of the following dimensions on this scaled drawing? _____ inches wide and _____ inches long.
A. 9.5; 20.5 B. 12.5; 22 C. 17;32 D. 25; 44

41. In a division of clerks and stenographers, 15 people are currently employed, 20% of whom are stenographers. 41.____
If management plans are to maintain the current number of stenographers, but to increase the clerical staff to the point where 12% of the total staff are stenographers, what is the MAXIMUM number of additional clerks that should be hired to meet these plans?
A. 3 B. 8 C. 10 D. 12

42. Suppose that a certain agency had a 2018 budget of $1,200,500. The 2019 budget was 7% higher than that of 2018, and the 2020 budget was 8% higher than that of 2019. 42.____
Of the following, which one is MOST NEARLY that agency's budget for 2020?
A. $1,177,624 B. $1,261,737 C. $1,265,575 D. $1,271,738

Questions 43-50.

DIRECTIONS: Your office keeps a file card record of the work assignments for all the employees in a certain bureau. On each card is the employee's name, a work assignment code number, and the date of this assignment. In this filing system, the employee's name is filed alphabetically, the work assignment code is filed numerically, and the date of assignment is filed chronologically (earliest date first).

Each of Questions 43 through 50 represents five cards to be filed, numbered (1) through (5) shown in Column I. Each card is made up of the employee's name, a work assignment code number shown in parentheses, and the date of this assignment. The cards are to be filed according to the following rules:

First: File in alphabetical order.
Second: When two or more cards have the same employee's name, file according to the work assignment number, beginning with the lowest number.
Third: When two or more cards have the same employee's name and same assignment number, file according to the assignment date beginning with earliest date.

Column II shows the cards arranged in four different orders. Pick the answer (A, B, C, or D) in Column II which shows the cards arranged correctly according to the above filing rules.

SAMPLE QUESTION:

		Column I		Column II
(1)	Cluney	(486503)	6/17/07	A. 2, 3, 4, 1, 5
(2)	Roster	(246611)	5/10/06	B. 2, 5, 1, 3, 4
(3)	Altool	(711433)	10/15/07	C. 3, 2, 1, 4, 5
(4)	Cluney	(527610)	12/18/06	D. 3, 5, 1, 4, 2
(5)	Cluney	(486500)	4/8/07	

The CORRECT way to file the cards is:

(3)	Altool	(711433)	10/15/07
(5)	Cluney	(486500)	4/8/07
(1)	Cluney	(486503)	6/17/07
(4)	Cluney	(527610)	12/18/06
(2)	Roster	(246611)	5/10/06

The correct filing order is shown by the numbers in front of each name (3, 5, 1, 4, 2). The answer to the sample question is the letter in Column II in front of the numbers 3, 5, 1, 4, 2. This answer is D.

			Column I		Column II	
43.	(1)	Prichard	(013469)	4/6/06	A. 5, 4, 3, 2, 1	43.____
	(2)	Parks	(678941)	2/7/06	B. 1, 2, 5, 3, 4	
	(3)	Williams	(551467)	3/6/05	C. 2, 1, 5, 3, 4	
	(4)	Wilson	(551466)	8/9/02	D. 1, 5, 4, 3, 2	
	(5)	Stanhope	(300014)	8/9/02		
44.	(1)	Ridgeway	(623809)	8/11/06	A. 5, 1, 3, 4, 2	44.____
	(2)	Travers	(305439)	4/5/02	B. 5, 1, 3, 2, 4	
	(3)	Tayler	(818134)	7/5/03	C. 1, 5, 3, 2, 4	
	(4)	Travers	(305349)	5/6/05	D. 1, 5, 4, 2, 3	
	(5)	Ridgeway	(62309)	10/9/06		
45.	(1)	Jaffe	(384737)	2/19/06	A. 3, 5, 2, 4, 1	45.____
	(2)	Inez	(859176)	8/8/07	B. 3, 5, 2, 1, 4	
	(3)	Ingrahm	(946460)	8/6/04	C. 2, 3, 5, 1, 4	
	(4)	Karp	(256146)	5/5/05	D. 2, 3, 5, 4, 1	
	(5)	Ingrahm	(946460)	6/4/05		
46.	(1)	Marrano	(369421)	7/24/04	A. 1, 5, 3, 4, 2	46.____
	(2)	Marks	(652910)	2/23/06	B. 3, 5, 4, 2, 1	
	(3)	Netto	(556772)	3/10/07	C. 2, 4, 1, 5, 3	
	(4)	Marks	(652901)	2/17/07	D. 4, 2, 1, 5, 3	
	(5)	Netto	(556772)	6/17/05		
47.	(1)	Abernathy	(712467)	6/23/05	A. 5, 3, 1, 2, 4	47.____
	(2)	Acevedo	(680262)	6/23/03	B. 5, 4, 2, 3, 1	
	(3)	Aaron	(967647)	1/17/04	C. 1, 3, 5, 2, 4	
	(4)	Acevedo	(680622)	5/14/02	D. 2, 4, 1, 5, 3	
	(5)	Aaron	(967647)	4/1/00		

48.	(1)	Simon	(645219)	8/19/05	A. 4, 1, 2, 5, 3	48.____
	(2)	Simon	(645219)	9/2/03	B. 4, 5, 2, 1, 3	
	(3)	Simons	(645218)	7/7/05	C. 3, 5, 2, 1, 4	
	(4)	Simms	(646439)	10/12/06	D. 5, 1, 2, 3, 4	
	(5)	Simon	(645219)	10/16/02		
49.	(1)	Rappaport	(312230)	6/11/06	A. 4, 3, 1, 2, 5	49.____
	(2)	Rascio	(777510)	2/9/05	B. 4, 3, 1, 5, 2	
	(3)	Rappaport	(312230)	7/3/02	C. 3, 4, 1, 5, 2	
	(4)	Rapaport	(312330)	9/6/05	D. 5, 2, 4, 3, 1	
	(5)	Rascio	(777501)	7/7/05		
50.	(1)	Johnson	(843250)	6/8/02	A. 1, 3, 2, 4, 5	50.____
	(2)	Johnson	(843205)	4/3/05	B. 1, 3, 2, 5, 4	
	(3)	Johnson	(843205)	8/6/02	C. 3, 2, 1, 4, 5	
	(4)	Johnson	(843602)	3/8/06	D. 3, 2, 1, 5, 4	
	(5)	Johnson	(843602)	8/3/05		

KEY (CORRECT ANSWERS)

1.	D	11.	B	21.	C	31.	B	41.	C
2.	A	12.	A	22.	A	32.	B	42.	D
3.	C	13.	C	23.	D	33.	A	43.	C
4.	C	14.	C	24.	B	34.	C	44.	A
5.	C	15.	A	25.	D	35.	B	45.	C
6.	A	16.	D	26.	C	36.	A	46.	D
7.	B	17.	A	27.	B	37.	C	47.	A
8.	C	18.	C	28.	C	38.	B	48.	B
9.	D	19.	D	29.	A	39.	B	49.	B
10.	A	20.	B	30.	C	40.	B	50.	D

EXAMINATION SECTION

TEST 1

DIRECTIONS: Each question or incomplete statement is followed by several suggested answers or completions. Select the one that BEST answers the question or completes the statement. *PRINT THE LETTER OF THE CORRECT ANSWER IN THE SPACE AT THE RIGHT.*

1. An executive assigns A, the head of a staff unit, to devise plans for reducing the delay in submittal of reports by a local agency headed by C. The reports are under the supervision of C's subordinate line official B with whom A is to deal directly. In his investigation, A finds: (1) the reasons for the delay; and (2) poor practices which have either been overlooked or condoned by line official B. 1.____
   Of the following courses of action A could take, the BEST one would be to
   A. develop recommendations with line official B with regard to reducing the delay and correcting the poor practice and then report fully to his own executive
   B. discuss the findings with C in an attempt to correct the situation before making any formal report on the poor practices
   C. report both findings to his executive, attaching the explanation offered by C
   D. report to his executive on the first finding and discuss the second in a friendly way with line official B
   E. report the first finding to his executive, ignoring the second until his opinion is requested

2. Drafts of a proposed policy, prepared by a staff committee, are circulated to ten member of the field staff of the organization by route slips with a request for comments within two weeks. Two members of the field staff make extensive comments, four offer editorial suggestions, and the remainder make minor favorable comments. Shortly after, it found that the statement needs considerable revision by the field staff. 2.____
   Of the following possible reasons for the original failure of the field staff to identify difficulties, the MOST likely is that the
   A. field staff did not take sufficient time to review the manual
   B. field staff had not been advised of the type of contribution expected
   C. low morale of the field staff prevented their showing interest
   D. policy statement was too advanced for the staff
   E. staff committee was not sufficiently representative

3. Operator participation in management improvement work is LEAST likely to 3.____
   A. assure the use of best available management technique
   B. overcome the stigma of the outside expert
   C. place responsibility for improvement in the person who knows the job best
   D. simplify installation
   E. take advantage of the desire of most operators to seek self-improvement

4. In general, the morale of workers in an agency is MOST frequently and MOST significantly affected by the 4.____
   A. agency policies of organizational structure and operational procedures
   B. distance of the employee's job from his home community
   C. fringe benefits
   D. number of opportunities for advancement
   E. relationship with supervisors

5. Of the following, the PRIMARY function of a work distribution chart is to 5.____
   A. analyze the soundness of existing divisions of labor
   B. eliminate the unnecessary clerical detail
   C. establish better supervisory techniques
   D. simplify work methods
   E. weed out core functions

6. In analyzing a process chart, which one of the following should be asked FIRST? 6.____
   A. How B. When C. Where D. Who E. Why

7. Which one of the following is NOT an advantage of the interview method of collecting data? It 7.____
   A. enables interviewer to judge the person interviewed on such matters as general attitude, knowledge, etc.
   B. helps build up personal relations for later installation of changes
   C. is a flexible method that can be adjusted to changing circumstances
   D. permits the obtaining of *off the record* information
   E. produces more accurate information than other methods

8. Which one of the following may be defined as a *regularly recurring appraisal of the manner in which all elements of agency management are being carried out*? 8.____
   A. Functional survey
   B. Operations audit
   C. Organization survey
   D. Over-all survey
   E. Reconnaissance survey

9. An analysis of the flow of work in a department should begin with the _____ work. 9.____
   A. major routine
   B. minor routine
   C. supervisory
   D. technical
   E. unusual

10. Which method would MOST likely be used to get first-hand information on complaints from the public? 10.____
   A. Study of correspondence
   B. Study of work volume
   C. Tracing specific transactions through a series of steps
   D. Tracing use of forms
   E. Worker desk audit

11. People will generally produce the MOST if 11.____
   A. management exercises close supervision over the work
   B. there is strict discipline in the group
   C. they are happy in their work
   D. they feel involved in their work
   E. they follow *the one best way*

12. The normal analysis of which chart listed below is MOST closely related to organizational analysis? _____ chart. 12.____
   A. Layout
   B. Operation
   C. Process
   D. Work count
   E. Work distribution

13. The work count would be LEAST helpful in accomplishing which one of the following? 13.____
   A. Demonstrating personnel needs
   B. Improving the sequence of steps
   C. Measuring the value of a step
   D. Spotting bottlenecks
   E. Stimulating interest in work

14. Which one of the following seems LEAST useful as a guide in interviewing an employee in a procedure and methods survey? 14.____
   A. Explaining who you are and the purpose of your visit
   B. Having a general plan of what you intend to get from the interview
   C. Listening carefully and not interrupting
   D. Trying out his reactions to your ideas for improvements
   E. Trying to analyze his reasons for saying what he says

15. Which one of the following is an advantage of the questionnaire method of gathering facts as compared with the interview method? 15.____
   A. Different people may interpret the questions differently
   B. Less *off the record* information is given
   C. More time may be taken in order to give exact answers
   D. Personal relationships with the people involved are not established
   E. There is less need for follow-up

16. Which one of the following is generally NOT an advantage of the personal observation method of gathering facts? It 16.____
   A. enables staff to use *off the record* information if personally observed
   B. helps in developing valid recommendations
   C. helps the person making the observation acquire *know how* valuable for later installation and follow-up
   D. is economical in time and money
   E. may turn up other problems in need of solution

17. Which of the following would MOST often be the best way to minimize resistance to change? 17.____
   A. Break the news about the change gently to the people affected
   B. Increase the salary of the people affected by the change
   C. Let the people concerned participate at the decision to change

D. Notify all people concerned with the change, both orally and in writing
E. Stress the advantages of the new system

18. The functional organization chart 18.____
A. does not require periodic revision
B. includes a description of the duties of each organization segment
C. includes positions and titles for each organization segment
D. is the simplest type of organization chart
E. is used primarily by newly established agencies

19. The principle of span of control has frequently been said to be in conflict with the 19.____
A. principle of unity of command
B. principle that authority should be commensurate with responsibility
C. principle that like functions should be grouped into one unit
D. principle that the number of levels between the top of an organization and the bottom should be small
E. scalar principle

20. If an executive delegates to his subordinates authority to handle problems of a routine nature for which standard solutions have been established, he may expect that 20.____
A. fewer complaint will be received
B. he has made it more difficult for his subordinates to solve these problems
C. he has opened the way for confusion in his organization
D. there will be a lack of consistency in the methods applied to the solution of these problems
E. these routine problems will be handled efficiently and he will have more time for other non-routine work

21. Which of the following would MOST likely be achieved by a change in the basic organization structure from the *process* or *functional* type to the *purpose* or *product* type? 21.____
A. Easier recruitment of personnel in a tight labor market
B. Fixing responsibility at a lower level in the organization
C. Greater centralization
D. Greater economy
E. Greater professional development

22. Usually the MOST difficult problem in connection with a major reorganization is 22.____
A. adopting a pay plan to fit the new structure
B. bringing the organization manual up-to-date
C. determining the new organization structure
D. gaining acceptance of the new plan by the higher level employees
E. gaining acceptance of the new plan by the lower level employees

23. Which of the following statements MOST accurately describes the work of the chiefs of MOST staff divisions in departments? 23.____
Chiefs
   A. focus more on getting the job done than on how it is done
   B. are mostly interested in short-range results
   C. nearly always advise but rarely advise
   D. usually command or control but rarely advise
   E. provide service to the rest of the organization and/or assist the chief executive in planning and controlling operations

24. In determining the type of organization structure of an enterprise, the one factor that might be given relatively greater weight in a small organization than in a larger organization of the same nature is the 24.____
   A. geographical location of the enterprise
   B. individual capabilities of incumbents
   C. method of financing to be employed
   D. size of the area served
   E. type of activity engaged in

25. Functional foremanship differs MOST markedly from generally accepted principle of administration in that it advocates 25.____
   A. an unlimited span of control
   B. less delegation of responsibility
   C. more than one supervisor for an employee
   D. nonfunctional organization
   E. substitution of execution for planning

KEY (CORRECT ANSWERS)

1. A
2. B
3. A
4. E
5. A

6. E
7. E
8. B
9. A
10. A

11. D
12. E
13. B
14. D
15. C

16. D
17. C
18. B
19. D
20. E

21. B
22. D
23. E
24. B
25. C

TEST 2

DIRECTIONS: Each question or incomplete statement is followed by several suggested answers or completions. Select the one that BEST answers the question or completes the statement. *PRINT THE LETTER OF THE CORRECT ANSWER IN THE SPACE AT THE RIGHT.*

1. Decentralization of the authority to make decisions is a necessary result of increased complexity in an organization, but for the sake of efficiency and coordination of operations, such decentralization must be planned carefully. A good general rule is that 1.____
   A. any decision should be made at the lowest possible point in the organization where all the information and competence necessary for a sound decision are available
   B. any decision should be made at the highest possible point in the organization, thus guaranteeing the best decision
   C. any decision should be made at the lowest possible point in the organization, but always approved by management
   D. any decision should be made by management and referred to the proper subordinate for comment
   E. no decision should be made by any individual in the organization without approval by a superior

2. One drawback of converting a conventional consecutive filing system to a terminal digit filing system for a large installation is that 2.____
   A. conversion would be expensive in time and manpower
   B. conversion would prevent the proper use of recognized numeric classification systems, such as the Dewey decimal, in classifying files material
   C. responsibility for proper filing cannot be pinpointed in the terminal digit system
   D. the terminal digit system requires considerably more space than a normal filing system

3. The basic filing system that would ordinarily be employed in a large administrative headquarters unit is the _____ file system. 3.____
   A alphabetic
   B. chronological
   C. mnemonic
   D. retention
   E. subject classification

4. A records center is of benefit in a records management program PRIMARILY because 4.____
   A. all the records of the organization are kept in one place
   B. inactive records can be stored economically in less expense storage areas
   C. it provides a place where useless records can be housed at little or no cost to the organization

D. obsolete filing and storage equipment can be utilized out of view of the public
E. records analysts can examine an organization's files without affecting the unit's operation or upsetting the supervisors

5. In examining a number of different forms to see whether any could be combined or eliminated, which of the following would one be MOST likely to use? 5.____
A. Forms analysis sheet of recurring data
B. Forms control log
C. Forms design and approval request
D. Forms design and guide sheet
E. Numerical file

6. The MOST important reason for control of *bootleg* forms is that 6.____
A. they are more expensive than authorized forms
B. they are usually poorly designed
C. they can lead to unnecessary procedures
D. they cannot be reordered as easily as authorized terms
E. violation of rules and regulations should not be allowed

7. With a box design of a form, the caption title or question to be answered should be located in the _____ of the box. 7.____
A. center at the bottom
B. center at the top
C. lower left corner
D. lower right corner
E. upper left corner

8. A two-part snapout form would be MOST properly justified if 8.____
A. it is a cleaner operation
B. it is prepared ten times a week
C. it saves time in preparation
D. it is to be filled out by hand rather than by typewriter
E. proper registration is critical

9. When deciding whether or not to approve a request for a new form, which reference is normally MOST pertinent? 9.____
A. Alphabetical Forms File
B. Functional Forms File
C. Numerical Forms File
D. Project Completion Report
E. Records Retention Data

10. Which of the following statements BEST explains the significance of the famed Hawthorne Plant experiments? 10.____
They showed that
A. a large span of control leads to more production than a small span of control
B. morale has no relationship to production
C. personnel counseling is of relatively little importance in a going organization

D. the special attention received by a group in an experimental situation has a greater impact on production than changes in working conditions
E. there is a direct relationship between the amount of illumination and production

11. Which of the following would most often NOT result from a highly efficient management control system? 11.____
A. Facilitation of delegation
B. Highlighting of problem areas
C. Increase in willingness of people to experiment or to take calculated risks
D. Provision of an objective test of new ideas or new methods and procedures
E. Provision of information useful for revising objectives, programs, and operations

12. The PERT system is a 12.____
A. method for laying out office space on a modular basis utilizing prefabricated partitions
B. method of motivating personnel to be continuously alert and to improve their appearance
C. method of program planning and control using a network or flow plan
D. plan for expanding reporting techniques
E. simplified method of cost accounting

13. The term *management control* is MOST frequently used to mean 13.____
A. an objective and unemotional approach by management
B. coordinating the efforts of all parts of the organization
C. evaluation of results in relation to plan
D. giving clear, precise orders to subordinates
E. keeping unions from making managerial decisions

14. Which one of the following factors has the MOST bearing on the frequency with which a control report should be made? 14.____
A. Degree of specialization of the work
B. Degree of variability in activities
C. Expense of the report
D. Number of levels of supervision
E. Number of personnel involved

15. The value of statistical records is MAINLY dependent upon the 15.____
A. method of presenting the material
B. number of items used
C. range of cases sampled
D. reliability of the information used
E. time devoted to compiling the material

16. When a supervisor delegates an assignment, he should 16.____
    A. delegate his responsibility for the assignment
    B. make certain that the assignment is properly performed
    C. participate in the beginning and final stages of the assignment
    D. retail all authority needed to complete the assignment
    E oversee all stages of the assignment

17. Assume that the department in which you are employed has never given official sanction to a mid-afternoon coffee break. Some bureaus have it and others do not. In the latter case, some individuals merely absent themselves for about 15 minutes at 3 P.M. while others remain on the job despite the fatigue which seems to be common among all employees in this department at that time. 17.____
    The course of action which you should recommend, if possible, is to
    A. arrange a schedule of mid-afternoon coffee breaks for all employees
    B. forbid all employees to take a mid-afternoon coffee break
    C. permit each bureau to decide for itself whether or not it will have a coffee break
    D. require all employees who wish a coffee break to take a shorter lunch period
    E. arrange a poll to discover the consensus of the department

18. The one of the following which is LEAST important in the management of a suggestion program is 18.____
    A. giving awards which are of sufficient value to encourage competition
    B. securing full support from the department's officers and executives
    C. publicizing the program and the awards given
    D. holding special conferences to analyze and evaluate some of the suggestions needed
    E. providing suggestion boxes in numerous locations

19. The one of the following which is MOST likely to decrease morale is 19.____
    A. insistence on strict adherence to safety rules
    B. making each employee responsible for the tidiness of his work area
    C. overlooking evidence of hostility between groups of employees
    D. strong, aggressive leadership
    E. allocating work on the basis of personal knowledge of the abilities and interests of the member of the department

20. Assume that a certain office procedure has been standard practice for many years. 20.____
    When a new employee asks why this particular procedure is followed, the supervisor should FIRST
    A. explain that everyone does it that way
    B. explain the reason for the procedure
    C. inform him that it has always been done that way in that particular office
    D. tell him to try it for a while before asking questions
    E. tell him he has never thought about it that way

21. Several employees complain informally to their supervisor regarding some new procedures which have been instituted. 21.____
The supervisor should IMMEDIATELY
   A. explain that management is responsible
   B. state frankly that he had nothing to do with it
   C. refer the matter to the methods analyst
   D. tell the employees to submit their complaint as a formal grievance
   E. investigate the complaint

22. A new employee asks his supervisor how he is doing. Actually, he is not doing well in some phases of the job, but it is felt that he will learn in time. 22.____
The BEST response for the supervisor to make is:
   A. Some things you are doing well, and in others I am sure you will improve.
   B. Wait until the end of your probation period when we will discuss this matter.
   C. You are not doing too well.
   D. You are doing very well.
   E. I'll be able to tell you when I go over your record.

23. The PRINCIPAL aim of a supervisor is to 23.____
   A. act as liaison between employee and management
   B. get the work done
   C. keep up morale
   D. train his subordinates
   E. become chief of the department

24. When the work of two bureaus must be coordinated, direct contact between the subordinates in each bureau who are working on the problem is 24.____
   A. *bad*, because it violates the chain of command
   B. *bad*, because they do not have authority to make decisions
   C. *good*, because it enable quicker results
   D. *good*, because it relieves their superiors of any responsibilities
   E. *bad*, because they may work at cross purposes

25. Of the following, the organization defect which can be ascertained MOST readily merely by analyzing an accurate and well-drawn organization chart is 25.____
   A. ineffectiveness of an activity
   B. improper span of control
   C. inappropriate assignment of functions
   D. poor supervision
   E. unlawful delegation of authority

KEY (CORRECT ANSWERS)

1.	A	11.	C
2.	A	12.	C
3.	E	13.	C
4.	B	14.	B
5.	A	15.	D
6.	C	16.	B
7.	E	17.	A
8.	E	18.	E
9.	B	19.	C
10.	D	20.	B

21.	E
22.	A
23.	B
24.	C
25.	B

EXAMINATION SECTION

TEST 1

DIRECTIONS: Each question or incomplete statement is followed by several suggested answers or completions. Select the one that BEST answers the question or completes the statement. *PRINT THE LETTER OF THE CORRECT ANSWER IN THE SPACE AT THE RIGHT.*

1. The one of the following which BEST characterizes an agency in which delegation of authority is practiced on an organization-wide level is that the agency is 1.____
   A. autocratic
   B. authoritarian
   C. centralized
   D. decentralized

2. The concept of the *chain of command* is MOST similar to which one of the following concepts? 2.____
   A. Span of control
   B. Matrix or task-force organization
   C. Scalar principle
   D. Functional departmentation

3. The one of the following techniques which is NOT conducive to the establishment of an effective working relationship between employees and supervisors is 3.____
   A. periodic discussion of job performance with employees
   B. listening to employees when they discuss their job difficulties
   C. observation of employees on the job, in both individual and group situations, in order to help them with job performance
   D. treating all employees the same with respect to job performance and individual behavior

4. Which of the following is a valid, commonly-raised objection to the establishment of work standards for office clerical workers? 4.____
   A. Routine clerical work is not subject to accurate measurement.
   B. Clerical work standards can only lower employee morale by creating undue pressure to produce work rapidly.
   C. Work standards are not effective tools for planning, scheduling, and routing clerical work.
   D. Some phases of many clerical jobs, such as telephone answering or information gathering, cannot be readily or accurately measured.

5. Of the following, the feature which is LEAST characteristic of almost all successful staff relationships with line managers is that the staff employee 5.____
   A. is primarily a representative of his supervisor
   B. receives a salary at least equal to the average salary of his supervisor's direct line subordinates
   C. relies largely on persuasion to get his ideas put into effect
   D. is prepared to submerge his own personality and his own desire for recognition and see others often receive more recognition than he receives

6. The one of the following systems which has, as its principal objective, the storage of items in files so that they may be readily found when needed is called 6.____
   A. information retrieval
   B. simulation
   C. critical path
   D. PERT

7. A detailed description of the steps to be taken in order to accomplish a job is MOST appropriately called a 7.____
   A. policy
   B. rule
   C. procedure
   D. principle

8. In choosing the best place in the executive hierarchy to which to assign the task of making a certain type of decision, which one of the following should normally be LEAST important? 8.____
   A. Who knows the facts on which the decision will be based, or who can obtain them most readily?
   B. Who has the most adequate supply of current forms on which the decision is normally recorded?
   C. Who has the capacity to make sound decisions?
   D. How significant is the decision?

9. Of the following, the action which is LEAST likely to be either expressed or implied every time a manager delegates work to a subordinate is that the manager 9.____
   A. creates a need for a new class of positions
   B. indicates what work the subordinate is to do
   C. grants the subordinate some authority
   D. creates an obligation for the subordinate who accepts the work to try to complete it

10. Of the following, the LEAST appropriate use of organizational charts is to 10.____
    A. depict standard operating procedures
    B. indicate lines of responsibility
    C. indicate the relative level of key positions
    D. portray organizations graphically

11. The one of the following considerations which is generally LEAST important in deciding whether to automate a management operation by using a computer is whether the computer 11.____
    A. possesses a suitable array of programmed actions that might be taken
    B. can draw upon available data for information as to which alternative is best
    C. is already familiar to the staff of the organization
    D. can issue findings in a way that will facilitate the decision-making process

12. In evaluating a proposal to establish a library in your agency, it is generally considered LEAST necessary to determine 12.____
    A. the average time staff members spend on preparatory research when assigned to projects
    B. how often junior professional and technical staff members are sent out to *look something up* in a local library
    C. how much time and money agency executives devote to telephoning around the country seeking information before making decisions
    D. the quality of the research done by executives and scientists in the agency

13. In determining the number and type of tasks that should be combined into a single job, the one of the following which is normally the LEAST useful factor to consider is the 13.____
    A. benefit of functional specialization
    B. benefit of tall pyramid organization structures in increasing decentralization
    C. need for coordination of tasks with each other
    D. effect of the tasks assigned on the morale of the employee

14. Of the following, the one which is LEAST likely to be an objective of systems and procedures analysis is to 14.____
    A. eliminate as many unessential forms and records as feasible
    B. simplify forms in content and method of preparation
    C. mechanize repetitive, routine tasks
    D. expand as many of the forms as possible

15. A specific managerial function encompasses all of the following: The establishment of an intentional structure of roles through determination and enumeration of the activities required to achieve the goals of an enterprise and each part of it, the grouping of these activities, the assignment of such groups of activities to a manager, the delegation of authority to carry them out, and provision for coordination of authority and informational relationships horizontally and vertically in the organization structure. 15.____
    Of the following, the MOST appropriate term for this entire managerial function is
    A. organizing B. directing C. controlling D. staffing

16. The optimum number of subordinates that a supervisor can supervise effectively generally tends to vary INVERSELY with the 16.____
    A. percentage of the supervisor's time devoted to supervision rather than operations
    B. repetition of activities
    C. degree of centralization of decision-making within the supervisor's unit
    D. ability of subordinates

17. Under certain circumstances, a top manager may desire to strengthen the position of his staff people by granting them concurring authority, so that no action may be taken in a functional area by subordinate line officials until a designated staff employee agrees to the action. For example, office manages may have to get the approval of the agency personnel officer before hiring a new employee. 17.____
This approach is likely to be MOST valid under which one of the following conditions?
   A. The top manager refrains from indicating the grounds on which the staff employee may grant or withhold his approval of line proposals.
   B. The point of view represented by the staff employee is particularly important, and the possible delay in action will not be serious.
   C. It is more important to fix specific accountability for failure to take appropriate action than for wrong actions taken.
   D. The top manager gives speed priority over prudence.

18. The inclusion of the reason why a superior in his written orders to his subordinates normally is MOST likely to 18.____
   A. encourage belief by the subordinates in the meaning and intent of the order
   B. be a waste of valuable time for both superior and subordinates
   C. be useful principally where the superior has no power to enforce the order
   D. discourage effective two-way communication between superior and subordinates

19. The one of the following which is generally LEAST justification for an administrator's search for alternative methods of attaining a given objective of the unit he heads is that such search 19.____
   A. always turns up a better method of attaining objectives than that currently in use
   B. helps to make certain that the best method has a chance to be found and evaluated
   C. helps to insure that his peers realize that the existing method of attaining the objective is not the best
   D. is a good way to train the unit's staff in the organization's operational procedures

20. *Managing-by-Objectives* tends to place PRINCIPAL emphasis upon which of the following? 20.____
   A. Use of primarily qualitative goals at all management levels
   B. Use of trait-appraisal systems based upon personality factors
   C. Use of primarily qualitative goals at lower management levels as contrasted with primarily quantitative goals at higher management levels
   D. Goals which are clear and verifiable

21. Which one of the following BEST identifies the two most important considerations which generally should determine the degree of management decentralization desirable in a given situation? The 21.____
    A. age of the subordinate executives to whom decisions may be delegated and the number of courses in management that they have completed
    B. number of skills and the competence possessed by subordinate executives and the distribution of the necessary information to the points of decision
    C. ratio of the salary of the superior executives to the salary of the subordinate executives and the number of titles on the executive staff
    D. number of titles in the executive staff and the distribution of information to those various titles

22. Which one of the following is generally LEAST likely to occur at mid-level management as a result of installing an electronic data processing system? 22.____
    A. The time that managers will be required to spend on the controlling function will increase.
    B. The number of contacts that managers will have with subordinates will increase.
    C. Additional time will be needed to train people for managerial positions.
    D. There will be an increase in the volume of information presented to managers for analysis.

23. The concept that the major source of managerial authority is derived from the subordinate's acceptance of the manager's power is MOST closely identified with 23.____
    A. Luther Gulick
    B. John D. Mooney
    C. Frederick W. Taylor
    D. Chester I. Barnard

24. The one of the following which is generally the principal objection to a pure *functional organization*, as compared with a pure *line organization*, is that 24.____
    A. there is a tendency to overload intermediate and supervisory management at each succeeding level of organization with wide and varied duties
    B. authority flows in an unbroken line from top management to the worker
    C. workers must often report to two or more supervisors
    D. there is a lack of specialization at the supervisory level

25. The appraisal of subordinates and their performance is an integral part of the supervisor's job. There is wide agreement that several basic principles must be taken into account by supervisors involved in the appraisal process in order to perform this function correctly. 25.____
    The one of the following statements which LEAST represents a basic principle of the appraisal process is:
    Appraisal(s)
    A. should be based more on performance of definite tasks than on personality considerations
    B. of long-range potential should rely most heavily on subjective judgment of that potential

C. involves the use of value judgments by the supervisor and does, therefore, require reference to pre-established standards
D. should aim at emphasizing subordinates' strengths rather than weaknesses

26. Of the following, the INITIAL step in the decision-making procedure normally is 26.____
A. evaluation of alternatives
B. implementing the chosen course of action
C. listing potential solutions
D. diagnosis and problem definition

27. Management textbooks are LEAST likely to define coordination as 27.____
A. a concern for harmonious and unified action directed toward a common objective
B. the essence of management, since the basic purpose of management is the achievement of harmony of individual effort toward the accomplishment of group goals
C. the orderly arrangement of group effort to provide unity of action in pursuit of common purpose
D. the transmittal of messages from senders to receivers, involving acts of persuasion of regulation, or simply the rendering of information

28. A number of important assumptions underlie the modern human relations approach to management and administration. 28.____
The one of the following which is NOT an assumption integral to the human relations school of thought is that
A. employee participation is essential to higher productivity
B. employees are motivated solely by monetary factors
C. teamwork is indispensable for organization growth and survival
D. free-flow communications must be established and maintained for organizational effectiveness

29. Of the following, the MAIN purpose of systematic manpower planning is to 29.____
A. analyze the levels of skill needed by each worker
B. analyze causes of current vacancies, such as resignations, discharges, retirements, transfers, or promotions
C. save money by eliminating useless jobs
D. provide for the continuous and proper staffing of the workforce

30. A Planning-Programming-Budget System (PPBS) is PRIMARILY intended to do which of the following? 30.____
A. Improve control through a budgeting-by-line-item system
B. Plan and program budgets by objective rather than by function
C. Raise money for social welfare programs
D. Reduce budgets by planning and programming unspent funds

KEY (CORRECT ANSWERS)

1.	D	11.	C	21.	B
2.	C	12.	D	22.	A
3.	D	13.	B	23.	D
4.	D	14.	D	24.	C
5.	B	15.	A	25.	B
6.	A	16.	C	26.	D
7.	C	17.	B	27.	D
8.	B	18.	A	28.	B
9.	A	19.	B	29.	D
10.	A	20.	D	30.	B

TEST 2

DIRECTIONS: Each question or incomplete statement is followed by several suggested answers or completions. Select the one that BEST answers the question or completes the statement. *PRINT THE LETTER OF THE CORRECT ANSWER IN THE SPACE AT THE RIGHT.*

1. An administrative office is designed so that several administrative associates can log on to Microsoft Outlook and use an e-mail inbox that syncs in real time. Each associate can also send jobs to a central office printer. This is an example of 1.____
   A. network connectivity
   B. cloud connectivity
   C. office integration
   D. employee training

2. In the planning of office space for the various bureaus and divisions of an agency, the one of the following arrangements which is generally considered to be MOST desirable in a conventional layout is to 2.____
   A. locate offices where employees do close and tedious work, such as accounting, and also offices of high-level executives away from windows so that distractions will be minimal
   B. locate *housekeeping* offices such as data processing and the mailroom very close to the high executive offices to increase convenience for the executives
   C. locate departments so that the work flow proceeds in an uninterrupted manner
   D. centralize the executive suite for maximum availability and public exposure

3. Generally, the one of the following that is LEAST likely to be an essential step in a records retention plan is 3.____
   A. storing inactive records
   B. checking for accuracy of all records to be retained
   C. classification of all records
   D. making an inventory of all agency records

4. The PRINCIPAL asset of an office layout diagram, as contrasted with the more abstract organization charts and flowcharts, is that an office layout diagram is 4.____
   A. more readily adaptable to strictly conceptual studies
   B. pictorial and therefore easier to understand
   C. suitable for showing both manual and machine processing operations, whereas organization charts and flowcharts may only be used for manual processing operations
   D. better suited for summarizing the number of work units produced at each step

5. One of the assistants whom you supervise displays apparent familiarity toward a businessman who deals with your agency. This assistant spends more time with this person than the nature of his business would warrant, and you have observed that they are occasionally seen leaving the office together for lunch. In several instances, when this businessman comes into the office and this assistant is not at his desk, the businessman will not deal with any other staff member but will, instead, leave the office and return later when that particular employee is available. 5.____
Of the following courses of action, the FIRST one you should take is to
   A. audit the agency's books and records pertaining to this businessman
   B. rebuke the assistant for unprofessional conduct at the next staff meeting and warn him of disciplinary action if the practice is not discontinued forthwith
   C. advise your agency head of the action by the businessman and the assistant that has been described in the above paragraph
   D. reassign the assistant to duties that will not bring him into contact with any businessman

6. The one of the following factors which generally is the BEST justification for keeping higher inventories of supplies and equipment is an expected 6.____
   A. decline in demand
   B. price increase
   C. decline in prices
   D. increase in interest charges and storage costs

7. Statistical sampling is often used in administrative operations PRIMARILY because it enables 7.____
   A. administrators to determine the characteristics of appointed or elected officials
   B. decisions to be made based on mathematical and scientific fact
   C. courses of action to be determined by scientifically-based computer programs
   D. useful predictions to be made from relatively small samples

8. According to United States Department of Labor figures, the PRINCIPAL source of disabling injuries to office workers is 8.____
   A. flying objects and falling objects
   B. striking against equipment
   C. falls and slips
   D. handling materials

9. To expedite the processing of applications issued by your agency, you ask your assistant to design a form that will be used by your typists. After several discussions, he presents you with a draft that requires the typist to use 23 tabular-stop positions. 9.____
Such a form would PROBABLY be considered
   A. *undesirable*; typists would now have to soft-roll the platen to make the typing fall on the lines
   B. *desirable*; the fill-in operation by typists would be speeded up

C. *undesirable*; proper vertical alignment of data would be made difficult by the number of tabular-stop positions required
D. *desirable*; it would force the typists to utilize the tabular-stop device

Question 10.

DIRECTIONS: Following are five general instructions to file clerks which might appear in the proposed filing manual for an agency.

I. Follow instructions generally; if you have a suggestion for improvement in the filing methods, install it after notifying the file supervisor who will duly authorize a change in the manual.
II. You may discuss the contents of files with fellow employees or outsiders, but do NOT give papers from the file to any person whose duties have no relation to the material requested.
III. All special instructions must be given by the file supervisor. Any problems that arise outside the regular routine of filing must be decided by the file supervisor, not by a fellow clerk.
IV. You will not be held responsible for your own errors; thus, refrain from asking other workers for instructions. No one is more interested in helping you in your training than your file supervisor.
V. Speed is the first essential in filing; make it your primary consideration—quick finding of filed material is the real test of your efficiency.

10. Which of the choices listed below BEST identifies those of the above statements that should or should not be followed by agencies in the functioning of their filing sections? 10.____
Instruction(s) _____ should be followed; instructions _____ should not be followed.
A. I, II, III; IV, V
B. III; I, II, IV, V
C. II, IV; I, III, V
D. I, III; II, IV, V

11. Listed below are five steps in the process of staffing: 11.____
I. Authorization for staffing
II. Manpower planning
III. Development of applicant sources
IV. Evaluation of applicants
V. Employment decisions and offers
The one of the following sequences which is generally the MOST logical arrangement of the above steps is:
A. I, II, III, IV, V
B. II, I, III, IV, V
C. III, I, II, IV, V
D. II, III, I, IV, V

12. Job enrichment is LEAST likely to lead to 12.____
A. fewer employee grievances
B. increased employee productivity
C. people acting as adjuncts of increased automation
D. increased employee morale

13. Of the following, programmed instruction would usually be MOST effective in teaching 13.____
    A. principles of decision-making
    B. technical skills and knowledge
    C. good judgment
    D. executive management ability

14. Assume that a group has been working effectively with a contributing nonconformist in its midst. 14.____
    The BEST of the following reasons for the group to retain the nonconformist generally is that
    A. nonconformists stimulate groups to think
    B. he may be their boss some day
    C. nonconformists usually are fun to work with
    D. another nonconformist will usurp his role

15. The *grievance-arbitration* process involves systematic union-management deliberation regarding a complaint that work- or contract-related. 15.____
    An outcome that does NOT result from this process is
    A. a communications channel from the rank-and-file workers to higher management is developed or improved
    B. the contract is immediately changed to provide justice for both parties
    C. both labor and management identify those parts of the contract that need to be clarified and modified in subsequent negotiations
    D. the language of the agreement is informally translated into understandable terms for the parties bound by it

16. In government, job evaluation is the process of determining the relative worth of the various jobs in an organization so that differential wages can be paid. 16.____
    Job evaluation is based on several basic assumptions.
    Of the assumptions listed below, the MOST questionable is that
    A. the cash payments in government should be substantially higher than those in local private industry
    B. it is logical to pay the most for jobs that contribute most to the organization
    C. people feel more fairly treated if wages are based on the relative worth of their jobs
    D. the best way to achieve the goals of the enterprise is to maintain a wage structure based on job worth

17. Of the following, the training method that normally provides the instructor with the LEAST *feedback* from the trainees is 17.____
    A. the lecture method
    B. the conference method
    C. simulation or gaming techniques
    D. seminar instruction

18. Insufficient and inappropriate delegation of work assignments is MOST often the fault of 18.____
    A. subordinates who are unwilling to accept responsibility for their own mistakes
    B. a paternal attitude on the part of management

C. the immediate supervisor
D. subordinates who are too willing to take on extra responsibility

19. As contrasted with expense budgets, capital budgets are MORE likely to 19.____
A. be used for construction of physical facilities
B. be designed for a shorter time period
C. include personal service expenditures
D. include fringe benefits

20. During the first quarter of a year, a division's production rate was 1.26 man-hours per work unit produced. For the second quarter of that year, all other factors (e.g., size of staff, character of work unit, etc.) remained constant, except that the manner of reporting production rate was changed to work units per man-hour instead of man-hours per work unit. During that second quarter, the unit's production rate was .89 work units per man-hour. 20.____
On the basis of the above information, it would be MOST NEARLY CORRECT to conclude that the division's production rate during the second quarter was approximately _____ than during the first quarter.
A. 30% lower B. 10% lower C. 10% higher D. 30% higher

Questions 21-22.

DIRECTIONS: Questions 21 and 22 are to be answered on the basis of the following information.

The five bureaus within a department sent the following budget requests to the department head:

Bureau A: $10 million
Bureau B: $12 million
Bureau C: $18 million
Bureau D: $6 million
Bureau E: $4 million

After reviewing all of these requests, the department head decided to reduce these requests so that they would total only $40 million. He considered the following two options to accomplish this:

Option I: Reduce the requests of Bureaus A, B, and D by an equal dollar amount. Reduce the dollar amount request of Bureau C by 2½ times the dollar amount that he reduces the request of Bureau B. Reduce the dollar amount request of Bureau E by ½ of the dollar amount that he reduces the request of Bureau B.

Option II: First, reduce the dollar amount request of all five bureaus by 15%. Then, the remaining reduction required by the entire department would be achieved by further reducing the resulting budget requests of Bureaus B and C by an equal dollar amount each.

21. Under Option I, the dollar amount request for Bureau E, after reduction by the department head, would be MOST NEARLY _____ millions. 21._____
   A. $1²⁄₃ B. $2¹⁄₃ C. $3¹⁄₆ D. $3½

22. Under Option II, the dollar amount of the request of Bureau B, after both reductions were made by the department head, would be MOST NEARLY _____ millions. 22._____
   A. $8 B. $9 C. $10 D. $11

23. The Summary of finding of a long management report intended for typical manager should generally appear _____ the report. 23._____
   A. at the very beginning of
   B. at the end of the report
   C. throughout
   D. in the middle of

24. Of the following, the BIGGEST disadvantage in allowing a free flow of communications in an agency is that such a free flow 24._____
   A. decreases creativity
   B. increases the use of the *grapevine*
   C. lengthens the chain of command
   D. reduces the executive's power to direct the flow of information

25. A downward flow of authority in an organization is one example of _____ communications. 25._____
   A. horizontal B. informal C. circular D. vertical

26. Workers who belong to a cohesive group are generally thought to 26._____
   A. have more job-related anxieties than those who do not
   B. be less well-adjusted than those who do not
   C. derive little satisfaction from the group
   D. Conform to group norms more closely than those in noncohesive groups

27. The one of the following which BEST exemplifies negative motivation is 27._____
   A. a feeling on the part of the worker that the work is significant
   B. monetary rewards offered the worker for high levels of output
   C. reducing or withholding the worker's incentive rewards when performance is mediocre
   D. nonmonetary rewards given the worker, such as publicizing a good suggestion

28. Of the following, the one that would be MOST likely to block effective communication is 28._____
   A. concentration only on the issues at hand
   B. lack of interest or commitment
   C. use of written reports
   D. use of charts and graphs

29. Many functions formerly centralized in a department of personnel have been decentralized, in whole or in part, to operating agencies. 29.____
The one of the following personnel functions which has been LEAST decentralized is
   A. positive evaluation
   B. investigation of non-competitive employees
   C. investigation of competitive employees
   D. jurisdictional classification

30. In making a position analysis for a duties classification, the one of the following factors which MUST be considered is the _____ the incumbent. 30.____
   A. capabilities of
   B. qualifications of
   C. efficiency attained by
   D. responsibility assigned to

KEY (CORRECT ANSWERS)

1.	A	11.	B	21.	C
2.	C	12.	C	22.	B
3.	B	13.	B	23.	A
4.	B	14.	A	24.	D
5.	C	15.	B	25.	D
6.	B	16.	A	26.	D
7.	D	17.	A	27.	C
8.	C	18.	C	28.	B
9.	C	19.	A	29.	D
10.	B	20.	C	30.	D

EXAMINATION SECTION

TEST 1

DIRECTIONS: Each question or incomplete statement is followed by several suggested answers or completions. Select the one that BEST answers the question or completes the statement. *PRINT THE LETTER OF THE CORRECT ANSWER IN THE SPACE AT THE RIGHT.*

1. The number of subordinates that can be supervised directly by one person tends to 1.____
   A. *increase* as the level of supervision progresses from the first-line supervisory level to the management level
   B. *decrease* as the duties of the subordinates increase in difficulty and complexity
   C. *decrease* with an increase in the knowledge and experience of the subordinates
   D. *increase* as the physical distance between supervisor and subordinates, as well as between the individual subordinate, increases

2. A study of the supervision of employees in an agency reveals that the bureau chiefs are reluctant to delegate responsibility and authority to their assistants. 2.____
   This study is MOST likely to reveal, in addition, that
   A. the organizational structure of this agency should be centralized
   B. the bureau chiefs tend to spend too much of their time on minor aspects of their work
   C. the number of employees supervised by bureau chiefs is excessive
   D. significant deviations from planned performance are not called to the attention of the bureau chiefs

3. The delegation of responsibility and authority to subordinates by their superior generally does NOT 3.____
   A. facilitate a division of labor or the development of specialization
   B. permit the superior to carry out programs of work that exceed his immediate personal limits of physical energy and knowledge
   C. result in a downward transfer of work, both mental and manual
   D. involve a transfer of ultimate responsibility from superior to subordinate

4. Horizontal coordination is achieved when the various units of a bureau work with mutual harmony and assistance. 4.____
   The achievement of such coordination is generally made MORE difficult when the chief of a large bureau
   A. conducts periodic conferences with supervisors of his operating units
   B. delegates some of his coordinating tasks to a staff assistant
   C. increases the number of specialized units in his bureau and the degree of their specialization
   D. transfers subordinates from one to another of his operating units to broaden their understanding of the bureau's work

5. Some subdivision of work is imperative in large-scale operations. However, in subdividing work, the superior should adopt the methods that have the greatest number of advantages and the fewest disadvantages. 5.____
The one of the following that is MOST likely to result from subdivision of work is
A. measuring work performed by employees is made more difficult
B. authority and responsibility for performance of particular operations are not clearly defined
C. standardizing work processes is made more difficult
D. work is delayed in passing between employees and between operating units

6. In developing a system for controlling the production of a bureau, the bureau chief should give consideration to reducing the fluctuations in the bureau's work load. 6.____
Of the following, the technique that is generally LEAST helpful in reducing fluctuations in work load is]
A. staffing the bureau so that it can handle peak loads
B. maintaining a controlled backlog of work
C. regulating the order of steps in work processes
D. changing the order of steps in work processes

7. The flow of work in an organization may be divided and channeled according to either a serial method or a parallel method. Under the serial method, the work moves through a single channel with each job progressing step by step through various work stations where a worker at each station completes a particular step of the job. Under the parallel method, the jobs are distributed among a number of workers, each worker completing all the steps of a job. 7.____
The MOST accurate of the following statements regarding these two methods of dividing the flow of work is that
A. the training or break-in time necessary for workers to acquire processing skills is generally shorter under the parallel method
B. the serial method enables the workers to obtain a fuller understanding of the significance of their work
C. the parallel method tends to minimize the need for control devices to keep track of individual jobs in process
D. flexibility in the use of available staff is generally increased under the serial method

8. The executive who has immediate responsibility for a group of functions should have the right to decide what the structure of his organization shall be. 8.____
In making such decision, the executive should realize that
A. the lower the competence of a staff, the more important it is to maintain a sound organizational structure
B. the productivity of a competent staff will not be affected by an impairment in organizational structure
C. the productivity of a staff whose level of competency is low cannot be improved by an improvement in organizational structure
D. where there is a sound organizational structure there must of necessity be a sound organization

9. Of the following means that a bureau chief may utilize in training his understudy, the LEAST acceptable one is for him to 9.____
   A. give the understudy assignments which other employees find too difficult or unpleasant
   B. discuss with the understudy the important problems that confront the bureau chief
   C. rotate the assignments given the understudy
   D. give the understudy an opportunity to attend some of the meetings of bureau chiefs

10. Of the following practices and techniques that may be employed by the conference leader, the one that the conference leader should ordinarily AVOID is 10.____
   A. permitting certain participants to leave the conference to get back to their work when the discussion has reached the point where their special interests or qualifications are no longer involved
   B. encouraging the participants to take full written notes for later comparison with the minutes of the meeting
   C. helping a participant extricate himself from an awkward position in which the participant has placed himself by an ill-advised remark
   D. translating the technical remarks of a speaker for the benefit of some participants who would otherwise fail to grasp the meaning of the remarks

11. In assigning work to his subordinates, a supervisor is MOST likely to lose the respect of his subordinate if he 11.____
   A. reviews with a new employee the main points of an oral order issued to this employee
   B. issues written orders instead of oral orders when a subordinate has repeatedly failed to carry out oral orders
   C. gives oral orders regarding a task which the subordinate has performed satisfactorily in the past
   D. gives an oral order which he feels the subordinate will not carry out

12. Both Agency X and Agency Y have district offices in all areas of the city. In Agency X, the activities of the various districts are administered under centralized control, whereas in Agency U the activities of the various district offices are administered under decentralized control. 12.____
   The one of the following which is MORE characteristic of Agency X than of Agency Y is that in Agency X
   A. activities of the district offices can more readily be adapted to meet the problems of the district served
   B. there are greater opportunities for district administration to develop resourcefulness
   C. agency policies can be carried out with greater uniformity
   D. decisions are made by individuals closer to the points at which problems arise

13. Of the following training methods, the one that is generally MOST valuable in teaching employees new clerical skills is 13.____
   A. organized group discussion
   B. individual instruction on the job
   C. use of visual aids, such as charts and pictures
   D. supervised reading, research, and inspection

14. Department X maintains offices in each district of the city. Data gathered by the district offices are submitted monthly to the main office on a standard set of forms which are somewhat complicated. 14.____
   Of the following methods of issuing detailed instructions for filling out the forms properly, the one generally considered MOST acceptable is
   A. incorporating the instructions in the department's procedure manual
   B. including an instruction sheet with each package of blank forms sent to a district office
   C. printing the instructions on the back of each form
   D. conducting periodic staff conferences devoted exclusively to discussions of the proper method of filling out the form

15. The one of the following which is usually LEAST affected by an increase in the personnel of an organization is the 15.____
   A. problems of employee relationships
   B. average amount of work performed by an employee
   C. importance of coordinating the work of organizational units
   D. number of first-line supervisors required

16. As part of his program to simplify clerical procedures, the chief of the records management division has decided to make an analysis of the forms used by his agency and to establish a system of forms control. He has assigned the assistant bureau chief to perform the bulk of the work in connection with this project. This assistant will receive part-time help from four subordinate employees. 16.____
   Of the following actions the bureau chief may take in planning the work on this project, the MOST appropriate one is for him to
   A. have the plans drawn up by the assistant and then submitted for final approval to the four part-time subordinates before work on the project is begun
   B. have the assistant work with him in drawing up the plans and then present the plans to the four part-time subordinates for their comments
   C. join with the five employees as a committee to formulate the plans for the project
   D. prepare the plans himself and then submit the plans for approval to all five employees who are to work on the project

17. Bureau X is composed of several clerical units, each supervised by a unit head accountable to the bureau chief. Assume that the bureau chief has a special task for an employee of one of the clerical units and wishes to issue instructions directly to the employee regarding this task. 17.____

The LEAST appropriate of the following procedures for the bureau chief to follow is to
   A. issue the instructions to the employee without notifying the employee's unit head
   B. give the instructions to the employee in the presence of the unit head
   C. ask the unit head to send the employee to him for instructions on this special task
   D. tell the employee to inform his unit head of the bureau chief's instructions

18. A bureau chief has scheduled a conference with the unit heads in his bureau to obtain their views on a major problem confronting the bureau. 18.____
The LEAST appropriate action for him to take in conducting this conference is to
   A. present his own views of the solution of the problem before asking the unit heads for their opinions
   B. call upon a participant in the conference for information which this participant should have as part of his job
   C. weigh the opinions expressed at the conference in the light of the individual speaker's background and experience
   D. summarize briefly at the conclusion of the conference, the important points covered and the conclusions reached

19. Of the following, the GREATEST stress in selecting employees for office supervisory positions should ordinarily be placed on 19.____
   A. intelligence and educational background
   B. knowledge of the work and capacity for leadership
   C. sincere interest in the activities and objectives of the agency
   D. skill in performing the type of work to be supervised

20. The MOST acceptable of the following guides in preparing the specifications for a form is that 20.____
   A. when forms are to be printed on colored paper, the dark shades of colored paper should be used
   B. *tumble* or *head-to-foot* should be used if forms printed on both sides of the sheet are to be placed in binders with side binding
   C. provision for ballot-type entries should be made if items requiring *yes* or *no* entries are to appear on the form
   D. all-rag ledger paper rather than all-wood pulp bond paper should be used for forms which will receive little handling and will be kept for a short time

21. Suppose you are the chief of a bureau which contains several operating units. On one occasion you observe one of your unit heads severely reprimand a subordinate for violating a staff regulation. This subordinate has a good record for observing staff regulations, and you believe the severe reprimand will seriously undermine the morale of the employee. 21.____
Of the following, the BEST action for you to take in this situation is to
   A. call both the unit head and the subordinate into your office at the same time and have each present his views on the matter to you

B. refrain from intervening in this matter because the unit head may resent any interference
C. take the subordinate aside, inform him that the unit head had not intended to reprimand him several, and suggest that the matter be forgotten
D. discuss the matter with the unit head and suggest that he make some mitigating explanation to the subordinate

22. In addition to a report on its activities for the year, the one of the following items which it is MOST appropriate to include in an agency's annual report is 22.____
A. praise for each of the accomplishments of the agency during the year
B. pictures of agency personnel
C. history of the agency
D. descriptions of future activities and plans of the agency

23. Before transferring material from the active to the inactive files, the supervisor of the filing unit always consults the bureau heads directly concerned with the use of this material. 23.____
This practice by the supervisor is
A. *desirable*, chiefly because material that is no longer current for some bureaus may still be current for others
B. *undesirable*, chiefly because it can only lead to disagreement among the bureau heads consulted
C. *desirable*, chiefly because it is more economical to store records in transfer files than to keep them in the active files
D. *undesirable*, chiefly because the filing supervisor is expected to make his own decision

24. The determination of essential factors in a specific kind of work and of qualifications of a worker necessary for its competent performance is MOST accurately defined as 24.____
A. job analysis
B. micro-motion study
C. cost analysis
D. production control

25. In the clinical approach to disciplinary problems, attention is focused on the basic causes of which the overt relations are merely symptomatic rather than on the specific violations which have brought the employee unfavorable notice. 25.____
The MOST accurate implication of this quotation is that the clinical approach
A. places emphasis on the actual violation rather than on the cause of the violation
B. attempts to promote greater insight into the underlying factors which have led to the infractions
C. does not evaluate the justness and utility of applying a specific penalty in a given situation
D. avoids the necessity for disciplinarian action

26. The LEAST accurate of the following statements regarding the conduct of a conference is that 26.____
    A. when there is great disparity in the rank of the participants at a conference, the conference leader should ordinarily refrain from requesting an opinion point blank from a participant of relatively low rank
    B. when the aim of a conference is to obtain the opinion of a group of approximately the same rank, the rank of the conference leader should ordinarily not be too much higher than that of the participants
    C. in general, the chances that a conference will be fruitful are greatly increased if the conference leader's direct superior is one of the participants
    D. a top administrator invited to present a brief talk sponsoring a series of conferences for line supervisors should generally arrange to leave the conference as soon as appropriate after he has made his speech

27. In preparing a report for release to the general public, the bureau chief should GENERALLY present at the beginning of the report 27.____
    A. a description of the methods used in preparing the report
    B. anticipated criticism of the report and the answer to this criticism
    C. his conclusions and recommendations
    D. a bibliography of the sources used in preparing the report

28. Staff or functional supervision in an organization 28.____
    A. is least justified at the operational level
    B. is contrary to the principle of Unity of Command
    C. is more effective than authoritative supervision
    D. normally does not give the right to take direct disciplinary action

29. Suppose that you are the supervisor of Clerical Unit A in a city agency. Work processed in your unit is sent to Clerical Unit B for further processing. One of your subordinates complains to you that the supervisor of Clerical Unit B has been offering him unwarranted criticism of the method in which his work is performed. 29.____
    Of the following actions you may take, the MOST appropriate one for you to take FIRST is to
    A. request the supervisor of Clerical Unit B to meet with you and your subordinate to discuss this matter
    B. report this matter to this unit supervisor's immediate superior and request that this unsolicited criticism be discontinued
    C. obtain the facts from the subordinate and then discuss the matter with this unit supervisor
    D. tell your subordinate to refer the unit supervisor to you the next time he offers any criticism

30. This chart presents graphically a comparison of what is done and what is to be done. It is so ruled that each division of space represents both an amount of time and the quantity of work to be done during the particular unit of time. Horizontal lines drawn through these spaces show the relationship between the quantity of work actually done and that which is scheduled. 30.____

The chart referred to is known generally as a _____ chart.

A. progress or Gantt
B. job correlation
C. process or flow of work
D. Simo work simplification

31. The personnel survey is a systematic and reasonably exhaustive analysis and statement of the facts and forces in an organization which affect the relations between employees and management, and between employees and their work, followed by recommendations as to ways of developing better personnel policies and procedures. 31.____
On the basis of this statement, it is LEAST accurate to state that one of the purposes served by a personnel survey is to
   A. appraise operating efficiency through an objective study of methods of production and a statistical interpretation of the facts
   B. set forth items and causes of poor morale in an inclusive way and in their proper perspective
   C. secure the facts to determine whether there is need of a more progressive personnel policy in an organization where personnel work is as yet undeveloped
   D. evaluate the effectiveness of a personnel policy where a progressive personnel policy is already in operation

32. It is generally recognized that there is a relationship between the size of an organization's staff, the number of supervisory levels, and the span of control (number of workers assigned to a supervisor). 32.____
The MOST accurate of the following statements regarding the relationship of these three elements is that if the size of
   A. an organization's staff should remain unchanged and the span of control should increase, then the number of supervisory levels would tend to increase
   B. the staff should decrease and the number of levels of supervision should increase, then the span of control would tend to decrease
   C. staff should increase and the number of supervisory levels should remain unchanged, then the span of control would tend to decrease
   D. staff should increase and the span of control should decrease, then the number of supervisory levels would tend to decrease

Questions 33-35.

DIRECTIONS: Questions 33 through 35 are to be answered on the basis of the organization chart shown on the next page. This chart presents the organizational structure of a division in a hypothetical agency. Each box designates a position in the organizational structure of this division. The symbol in each box represents the name of the individual occupying the position designated by the box. Thus, the name of the head of this division is represented by the symbol 1A.

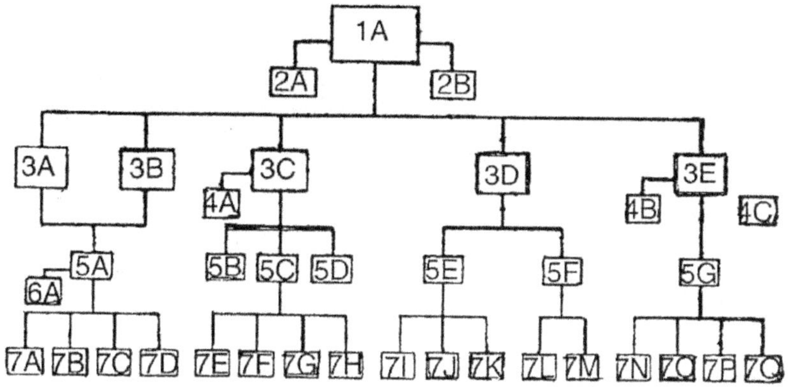

33. The one of the following who heads a subdivision which BEST illustrates in its organizational structure the characteristics of the pure line of organization is 33.____
    A. 3B B. 3C C. 3D D. 3E

34. The member of the organization who is MOST likely to receive conflicting orders because he is directly accountable to more than one superior is 34.____
    A. 5A B. 4A C. 5B D. 4C

35. Assume that 7K and 7P wish to exchange positions. Approval of this exchange must be obtained from each superior in the line of authority upward from 7K and from each superior in the line of authority extending upward from 7P. 35.____
    The one of the following who is NOT in a line of authority extending upward from either 7K or 7P is
    A. 1A B. 3E C. 5F D. 3D

KEY (CORRECT ANSWERS)

1.	B	11.	D	21.	D	31.	A
2.	B	12.	C	22.	D	32.	B
3.	D	13.	B	23.	A	33.	C
4.	C	14.	A/C	24.	A	34.	A
5.	D	15.	B	25.	B	35.	C
6.	A	16.	B	26.	C		
7.	C	17.	A	27.	C		
8.	A	18.	A	28.	D		
9.	A	19.	B	29.	C		
10.	B	20.	C	30.	A		

TEST 2

DIRECTIONS: Each question or incomplete statement is followed by several suggested answers or completions. Select the one that BEST answers the question or completes the statement. *PRINT THE LETTER OF THE CORRECT ANSWER IN THE SPACE AT THE RIGHT.*

1. Analysis and simplification of office procedures are functions that should be conducted in all offices and on a continuing basis. These functions may be performed by the line supervisor, by staff methods specialists, or by outside consultants on methods analysis. 1.____
An appraisal of these three methods of assigning responsibility for improving office procedures reveals that the LEAST accurate of the following statements is that
   A. outside consultants employed to simplify office procedures frequently bring with them a vast amount of previous experience as well as a fresh viewpoint
   B. line supervisors usually lack the special training which effective procedure analysis work requires
   C. continuity of effort and staff cooperation can better be secured by periodically employed consultants than by a permanent staff of methods analysts
   D. the reason line supervisors fail to keep procedures up to date is that the supervisor is too often overburdened with operating responsibilities

2. A man cannot serve two masters. 2.____
This statement emphasizes MOST the importance in an organization of
   A. span of control
   B. specialization of work
   C. delegation of authority
   D. unity of command

3. An important aid in good office management is knowledge on the part of subordinates of the significance of their work. 3.____
The possession of such knowledge by an employee will probably LEAST affect his
   A. interest in his work
   B. understanding of the relationship between the work of his unit and that of other units
   C. willingness to cooperate with other employees
   D. ability to undertake assignments requiring special skills

4. For mediocre executives who do not have a flair for positive administration, the implantation in subordinates of anxiety about job retention is a safe, if somewhat unimaginative, method of insuring a modicum of efficiency in the working organization. 4.____
Of the following, the MOST accurate statement according to this quotation is that
   A. implanting anxiety about job retention is a method usually employed by the mediocre executive to improve the efficiency of his organization

B. an organization will operate with at least some efficiency if employees realize that unsatisfactory work performance may subject them to dismissal
C. successful executives with a flair for positive administration relieve their subordinates of any concern for their job security
D. the implantation of anxiety about job security in subordinates should not be used as a method of improving efficiency

5. Savings of 20 percent or more in clerical operating costs can often be achieved by improvement of the physical conditions under which office work is performed. 5.____
In general, the MOST valid of the following statements regarding physical conditions is that
A. conference rooms should have more light than small rooms
B. the tops of desks should be glossy rather than dull
C. noise is reflected more by hard-surfaced materials than by soft or porous materials
D. yellow is a more desirable wall color for offices receiving an abundance of sunlight than for offices receiving little sunlight

6. To the executive who directs the complex and diverse operations of large organizational unit, the conference is an important and, at times, indispensable tool of management. The inexperienced executive may, however, ploy the conference for a purpose for which it is ill fitted. 6.____
Of the following, the LEAST use of the conference by the executive is to
A. reconcile conflicting views or interests
B. develop an understanding by all concerned of a policy already adopted
C. coordinate an activity involving several line supervisors
D. perform technical research on a specific project

7. In planning the layout of office space, the office supervisor should bear in mind that one large room is a more efficient operating unit than the same number of square feet split up into smaller rooms. 7.____
Of the following, the LEAST valid basis for the preceding statement is that in the large room
A. better light and ventilation are possible
B. flow of work between employees is more direct
C. supervision and control are more easily maintained
D. time and motion studies are easier to conduct

8. The one of the following companies which is BEST known as a manufacturer of filing cabinets and office furniture is 8.____
A. Pitney-Bowes, Inc. B. Dennison Manufacturing Co.
C. Wilson-Jones Co. D. Shaw-Walker Co.

9. The program used to deliver audio-visual office presentations is known as 9.____
A. PowerPoint B. Excel C. CGI D. Dreamweaver

10. The principles of scientific office management are MOST frequently applied by government office supervisors in 10.____
   A. maintaining flexibility in hiring and firing
   B. developing improved pay scales
   C. standardizing clerical practices and procedures
   D. revising organizational structure

11. The one of the following factors to which the bureau head should attach LEAST importance in deciding on the advisability of substituting machine for manual operations in a given area of office work is the 11.____
   A. need for accuracy in the work
   B. relative importance of the work
   C. speed with which the work must be completed
   D. volume of work

12. The clerk displayed a *rudimentary* knowledge of the principles of supervision. 12.____
The word *rudimentary* as used in this sentence means MOST NEARLY
   A. thorough B. elementary C. surprising D. commendable

13. This is an *integral* part of our program. 13.____
The word *integral* as used in this sentence means MOST NEARLY
   A. minor B. unknown C. essential D. well-developed

14. A *contiguous* office is one that is 14.____
   A. spacious B. rectangular in shape
   C. adjoining D. crowded

15. This program was *sanctioned* by the department head. 15.____
The word *sanctioned* as used in this sentence means MOST NEARLY
   A. devised B. approved C. modified D. rejected

16. The file clerk performed his work in a *perfunctory* manner. 16.____
The word *perfunctory* as used in this sentence means MOST NEARLY
   A. quiet B. orderly C. sullen D. indifferent

17. He did not *impugn* the reasons given for the change in policy. 17.____
The word *impugn* as used in this sentence means MOST NEARLY
   A. make insinuations against B. verify in whole or part
   C. volunteer support for D. overlook or ignore

18. The supervisor was unable to learn the identity of the *culpable* employee. 18.____
The word *culpable* as used in this sentence means MOST NEARLY
   A. inaccurate B. careless C. guilty D. dishonest

19. The announcement was made at a *propitious* time. 19.____
The word *propitious* as used in this sentence means MOST NEARLY
   A. unexpected B. busy C. favorable D. significant

20. He showed no *compunction* in carrying out this order. 20.____
The word *compunction* as used in this sentence means MOST NEARLY
A. feeling of remorse
B. hesitation or delay
C. tact or discretion
D. disposition to please

21. He acted in a *fiduciary* capacity. 21.____
The word *fiduciary* as used in this statement means MOST NEARLY
A. administrative or executive in nature
B. quasi-legal in nature
C. involving confidence or trust
D. requiring auditing or budgetary ability

22. To *temporize* means MOST NEARLY to 22.____
A. allay temporarily the fears of
B. render a temporary service
C. yield temporarily to prevailing opinion
D. react temperamentally

23. The new supervisor was *sanguine* about the prospects of success. 23.____
The word *sanguine* as used in this sentence means MOST NEARLY
A. uncertain
B. confident
C. pessimistic
D. excited

24. The supervisor was asked to *implement* the new policy. 24.____
The word *implemented* as used in this sentence means MOST NEARLY
A. explain
B. revise
C. delay the announcement of
D. carry into effect

25. The word *intimation* means MOST NEARLY 25.____
A. friendliness
B. an attempt to frighten
C. a difficult task
D. an indirect suggestion

26. Mr. Jones has a *penchant* for this type of work 26.____
The word *penchant* as used in this sentence means MOST NEARLY
A. record of achievement
B. unexplainable dislike
C. lack of aptitude
D. strong inclination

27. The speaker's comments were *desultory*. 27.____
The word *desultory* as used in this sentence means MOST NEARLY
A. inspiring
B. aimless
C. pertinent
D. rude

Questions 28-35.

DIRECTIONS: Questions 28 through 35 are to be answered SOLELY on the basis of the following chart which relates to the Investigation Division of Dept. X. This chart contains four curves which connect the points that show for each year the variations in percentage deviation from normal in the number of investigators, the number of clerical employee, the cost of personnel, and the number of cases processed for the period 2002-2012 inclusive. The year 2002 was designated as the normal year. The personnel of the Investigation Division consists of investigators and clerical employees only.

INVESTIGATION DIVISION, DEPARTMENT X

VARIATIONS IN NUMBER OF CASES PROCESSED, COST OF PERSONNEL NUMBER OF CLERICAL EMPLOYEES, AND NUMBER OF INVESTIGATORS FOR EACH YEAR FROM 2010 TO 2020 INCLUSIVE
(In percentages from normal)

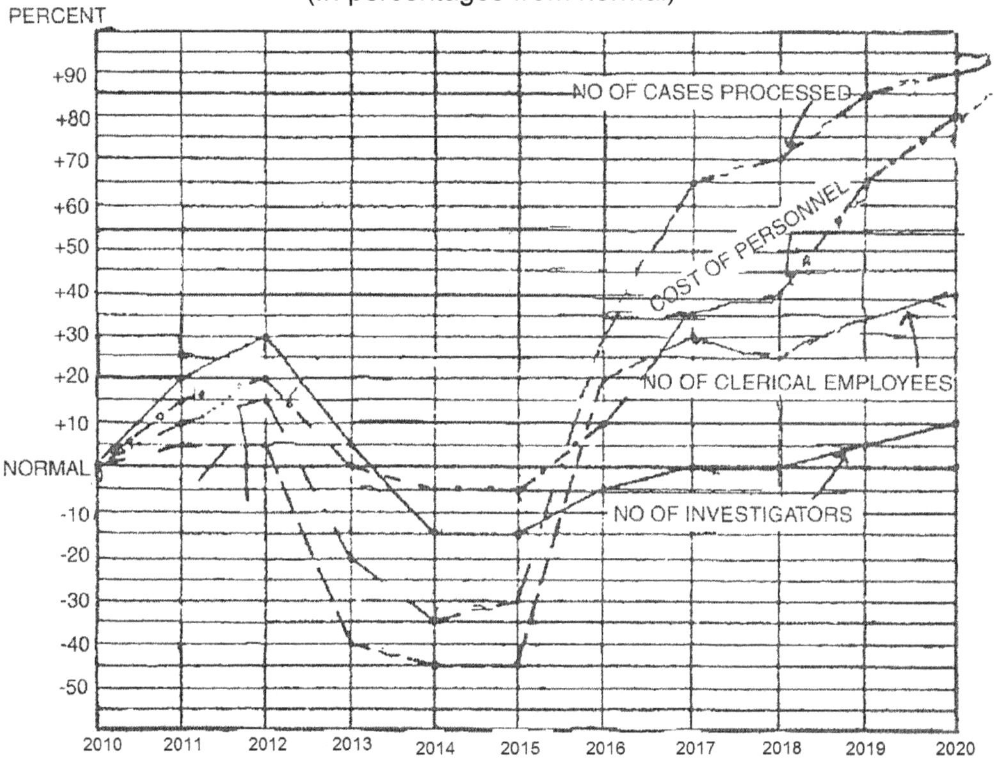

Example: If there were 80 clerical employees in the division in 2010 then the number of clerical employees in the division in 2017 was 104.

28. If 1,300 cases were processed by the division in 2014, then the number of cases processed in 2010 was 28.____
A. 2,000 B. 1,755 C. 2,145 D. 1,650

29. Of the following, the year in which there was no change in the size of the division's total staff from that of the preceding year is 29.____
A. 2013 B. 2014 C. 2017 D. 2019

30. Of the following, the year in which the size of the division's staff decreased MOST sharply from that of the preceding year is 30.____
A. 2013 B. 2014 C. 2015 D. 2016

31. An inspection of the chart discloses that the curve that fluctuates LEAST as determined by the average deviation from normal is the curve for the 31.____
A. number of cases processed
B. cost of personnel
C. number of clerical employees
D. number of investigators

32. A comparison of 2014 with 2020 reveals an increase in 2014 in the 32.____
A. cost of personnel for the division
B. number of cases processed per investigator
C. number of cases processed per clerical employee
D. number of clerical employees per investigator

33. If the personnel cost per case processed in 2010 was $12.30, then the personnel cost per case processed in 2020 was MOST NEARLY 33.____
A. $9.85 B. $10.95 C. $11.65 D. $13.85

34. Suppose that there was a total of 108 employees in the division in 2010 and a total of 125 employees in 2018. 34.____
On the basis of these figures, it is MOST accurate to state that the number of investigator employed in the division in 2018 was
A. 40 B. 57 C. 68 D. 85

35. It is predicted that the number of cases processed in 2021 will exceed the number processed in 2010 by exactly the same quantity that the number processed in 2012 exceeded that processed in 2019. It is also predicted that the personnel cost in 2021 will exceed the personnel cost in 2020 by exactly the same amount that the 2020 personnel cost exceeded that for 2019. On the basis of these predictions, it is MOST accurate to state that the personnel cost per case in 2021 will be 35.____
A. ten percent less than the personnel cost per case in 2020
B. exactly the same as the personnel cost per case in 2020
C. twice as much as the personnel cost per case in 2010
D. exactly the same as the personnel cost per case in 2010

KEY (CORRECT ANSWERS)

1.	C	11.	B	21.	C	31.	D
2.	D	12.	B	22.	C	32.	C
3.	D	13.	C	23.	B	33.	C
4.	B	14.	C	24.	D	34.	A
5.	C	15.	B	25.	B	35.	D
6.	D	16.	D	26.	D		
7.	D	17.	A	27.	B		
8.	D	18.	C	28.	A		
9.	A	19.	C	29.	B		
10.	C	20.	A	30.	A		

SUPERVISION, ADMINISTRATION, MANAGEMENT, AND ORGANIZATION

EXAMINATION SECTION

TEST 1

DIRECTIONS: Each question or incomplete statement is followed by several suggested answers or completions. Select the one that BEST answers the question or completes the statement. *PRINT THE LETTER OF THE CORRECT ANSWER IN THE SPACE AT THE RIGHT.*

1. In coaching a subordinate on the nature of decision-making, an executive would be right if he stated that the one of the following which is general the BEST definition of decision-making is: 1.____
   A. Choosing between alternatives
   B. Making diagnoses of feasible ends
   C. Making diagnoses of feasible means
   D. Comparing alternatives

2. Of the following, which one would be LEAST valid as a purpose of an organizational policy statement? 2.____
   To
   A. keep personnel from performing improper actions and functions on routine matters
   B. prevent the mishandling of non-routine matters
   C. provide management personnel with a tool that precludes the need for their use of judgment
   D. provide standard decisions and approaches in handling problems of a recurrent nature

3. Much has been written criticizing bureaucratic organizations. Current thinking on the subject is GENERALLY that 3.____
   A. bureaucracy is on the way out
   B. bureaucracy, though not perfect, is unlikely to be replaced
   C. bureaucratic organizations are most effective in dealing with constant change
   D. bureaucratic organizations are most effective when dealing with sophisticated customers or clients

4. The development of alternate plans as a major step in planning will normally result in the planner having several possible courses of action available. 4.____
   GENERALLY, this is
   A. *desirable*, since such development helps to determine the most suitable alternative and to provide for the unexpected
   B. *desirable*, since such development makes the use of planning premises and constraints unnecessary

C. *undesirable*, since the planners should formulate only one way of achieving given goals at a given time
D. *undesirable*, since such action restricts efforts to modify the planning to take advantage of opportunities

5. The technique of departmentation by task force includes the assigning of a team or task force to a definite project or block of work which extends from the beginning to the completing of a wanted and definite type and quantity of work. Of the following, the MOST important actor aiding the successful use of this technique *normally* is 5.____
A. having the task force relatively large, at least one hundred members
B. having a definite project termination date established
C. telling each task force member what his next assignment will be only after the current project ends
D. utilizing it only for projects that are regularly recurring

6. With respect to communication in small group settings such as may occur in business, government, and the military, it is generally TRUE that people usually derive more satisfaction and are usually more productive under conditions which 6.____
A. permit communication only with superiors
B. permit the minimum intragroup communication possible
C. are generally restricted by management
D. allow open communication among all group members

7. If an executive were asked to list some outstanding features of decentralization, which one of the following would NOT be such a feature? 7.____
Decentralization
A. provides decision-making experience for lower level managers
B. promotes uniformity of policy
C. is a relatively new concept in management
D. is similar to the belief in encouragement of free enterprise

8. Modern management experts have emphasized the importance of the informal organization in motivating employees to increase productivity. 8.____
Of the following, the characteristic which would have the MOST direct influence on employee motivation is the tendency of members of the informal organization to
A. resist change
B. establish their own norms
C. have similar outside interests
D. set substantially higher goals than those of management

9. According to leading management experts, the decision-making process contains separate and distinct steps that must be taken in an orderly sequence. 9.____
Of the following arrangements, which one is in CORRECT order?

A. I. Search for alternatives; II. diagnosis; III. comparison; IV. choice
B. I. Diagnose; II. comparison; III. search for alternatives; IV. choice
C. I. Diagnose; II. search for alternatives; III. comparison; IV. choice
D. I. Diagnose; II. search for alternatives; III. choice; IV. comparison

10. Of the following, the growth of professionalism in large organizations can PRIMARILY be expected to result in 10.____
A. greater equalization of power
B. increased authoritarianism
C. greater organizational disloyalty
D. increased promotion opportunities

11. Assume an executive carries out his responsibilities to his staff according to what is now known about managerial leadership. 11.____
Which of the following statements would MOST accurately reflect his assumptions about proper management?
A. Efficiency in operations results from allowing the human element to participate in a minimal way.
B. Efficient operation result from balancing work considerations with personnel considerations.
C. Efficient operation results from a workforce committed to its self-interest.
D. Efficient operation results from staff relationships that produce a friendly work climate.

12. Assume that an executive is called upon to conduct a management audit. To do this properly, he would have to take certain steps in a specific sequence. 12.____
Of the following steps, which step should this manager take FIRST?
A. Managerial performance must be surveyed.
B. A method of reporting must be established.
C. Management auditing procedures and documentation must be developed.
D. Criteria for the audit must be considered.

13. If a manager is required to conduct a scientific investigation of an organizational problem, the FIRST step he should take is to 13.____
A. state his assumptions about the problem
B. carry out a search for background information
C. choose the right approach to investigate the validity of his assumptions
D. define and state the problem

14. An executive would be right to assert that the principle of delegation states that decisions should be made PRIMARILY 14.____
A. by persons in an executive capacity qualified to make them
B. by persons in a non-executive capacity
C. at as low an organization level of authority as practicable
D. by the next lower level of authority

15. Of the following, which one is NOT regarded by management authorities as a FUNDAMENTAL characteristic of an *ideal* bureaucracy? 15.____
A. Division of labor and specialization
B. An established hierarchy
C. Decentralization of authority
D. A set of operating rules and regulations

16. As the number of subordinates in a manager's span of control increases, the ACTUAL number of possible relationships 16.____
A. increases disproportionately to the number of subordinates
B. increases in equal number to the number of subordinates
C. reaches a stable level
D. will first increase then slowly decrease

17. An executive's approach to controlling the activities of his subordinates concentrated on ends rather than means, and was diagnostic rather than punitive. 17.____
This manager may MOST properly be characterized as using the managerial technique of management-by-
A. exception B. objectives C. crisis D. default

18. In conducting a training session on the administrative control process, which of the following statements would be LEAST valid for an executive to make? 18.____
Controlling
A. requires checking upon assignments to see what is being done
B. involves comparing what is being done to what ought to be done
C. requires corrective action when what is being done does not meet expectations
D. occurs after all the other managerial processes have been performed

19. The "brainstorming" technique for creative solutions of management problems MOST generally consists of 19.____
A. bringing staff together in an exchange of a quantity of freewheeling ideas
B. isolating individual staff members to encourage thought
C. developing improved office procedures
D. preparation of written reports on complex problems

20. Computer systems hardware MOST often operates in relation to which one of the following steps in solving a data-processing problem? 20.____
A. Determining the problem
B. Defining and stating the problem
C. Implementing the programmed solution
D. Completing the documentation of every unexplored solution

21. There is a tendency in management to upgrade objectives. 21.____
This trend is generally regarded as
A. *desirable*; the urge to improve is demonstrated by adopting objectives that have been adjusted to provide improved service

B. *undesirable*; the typical manager searches for problems which obstruct his objectives
C. *desirable*; it is common for a manager to find that the details of an immediate operation have occupied so much of his time that he has lost sight of the basic overall objective
D. *undesirable*; efforts are wasted when they are expended on a mass of uncertain objectives, since the primary need of most organizations is a single target or several major ones

22. Of the following, it is generally LEAST effective for an executive to delegate authority where working conditions involve 22.____
    A. rules establishing normal operating procedures
    B. consistent methods of operation
    C. rapidly changing work standards
    D. complex technology

23. If an executive was explaining the difficulty of making decisions under *risk* conditions, he would be MOST accurate if he said that such decisions would be difficult to make when the decision maker has _____ information and experience and can expect _____ outcomes for each action. 23.____
    A. limited; many
    B. much; many
    C. much; few
    D. limited; few

24. If an executive were asked to list some outstanding features of centralized organization, which one of the following would be INCORRECT? 24.____
    Centralized organization
    A. lessens risks of errors by unskilled subordinates
    B. utilizes the skills of specialized experts at a central location
    C. produces uniformity of policy and non-uniformity of action
    D. enables closer control of operations than a decentralized set-up

25. It is possible for an organization's management to test whether or not the organization has a sound structure. 25.____
    Of the following, which one is NOT a test of soundness in an organization's structure?
    The
    A. ability to replace key personnel with minimum loss of effectiveness
    B. ability of information and decisions to flow more freely through the *grapevine* than through formal channels
    C. provision for orderly organizational growth with the ability to handle change as the need arises.

KEY (CORRECT ANSWERS)

1.	A	11.	B
2.	C	12.	D
3.	B	13.	D
4.	A	14.	C
5.	B	15.	C
6.	D	16.	A
7.	B	17.	B
8.	B	18.	D
9.	C	19.	A
10.	A	20.	C

21. A
22. C
23. A
24. C
25. B

TEST 2

DIRECTIONS: Each question or incomplete statement is followed by several suggested answers or completions. Select the one that BEST answers the question or completes the statement. *PRINT THE LETTER OF THE CORRECT ANSWER IN THE SPACE AT THE RIGHT.*

1. Management experts generally believe that computer-based management information systems (MIS) have greater potential for improving the process of management than any other development in recent decades. 1.____
The one of the following which MOST accurately describes the objectives of MIS is to
   A. provide information for decision-making on planning, initiating, and controlling the operations of the various units of the organization
   B. establish mechanization of routine functions such as clerical records, payroll, inventory, and accounts receivable in order to promote economy and efficiency
   C. computerize decision-making on planning, initiative, organizing, and controlling the operations of an organization
   D. provide accurate facts and figures on the various programs of the organization to be used for purposes of planning and research

2. The one of the following which is the BEST application on the *management-by-exception* principle is that this principle 2.____
   A. stimulates communication and aids in management of crisis situations, thus reducing the frequency of decision-making
   B. saves time and reserves top-management decisions only for crisis situations, thus reducing the frequency of decision-making
   C. stimulates communication, saves time, and reduces the frequency of decision-making
   D. is limited to crisis-management situations

3. It is generally recognized that each organization is dependent upon availability of qualified personnel. 3.____
Of the following, the MOST important factor affecting the availability of qualified people to each organization is
   A. innovations in technology and science
   B. the general decline in the educational levels of our population
   C. the rise of sentiment against racial discrimination
   D. pressure by organized community groups

4. A fundamental responsibility of all managers is to decide what physical facilities and equipment are needed to help attain basic goals. 4.____
Good planning for the purchase and use of equipment is seldom easy to do and is complicated MOST by the fact that
   A. organizations rarely have stable sources of supply
   B. nearly all managers tend to be better at personnel planning than at equipment planning

C. decisions concerning physical resources are made too often on a *crash basis* rather than under carefully prepared policies
D. legal rulings relative to depreciation fluctuate very frequently

5. In attempting to reconcile managerial objectives and an individual employee's goals, it is generally LEAST desirable for management to 5.____
   A. recognize the capacity of the individual to contribute toward realization of managerial goals
   B. encourage self-development of the employee to exceed minimum job performance
   C. consider an individual employee's work separately from other employees
   D. demonstrate that an employee advances only to the extent that he contributes directly to the accomplishment of stated goals

6. As a management tool for discovering individual training needs a job analysis would generally be of LEAST assistance in determining 6.____
   A. the performance requirements of individual jobs
   B. actual employee performance on the job
   C. acceptable standards of performance
   D. training needs for individual jobs

7. One of the major concerns of organizational managers today is how the spread of automation will affect them and the status of their positions. Realistically speaking, one can say that the MOST likely effect of our newer forms of highly automated technology on managers will be to 7.____
   A. make most top-level positions superfluous or obsolete
   B. reduce the importance of managerial work in general
   C. replace the work of managers with the work of technicians
   D. increase the importance of and demand for top managerial personnel

8. Which one of the following is LEAST likely to be an area or cause of trouble in the use of staff people (e.g., assistants to the administrator)? 8.____
   A. Misunderstanding of the role the staff people are supposed to play, as a result of vagueness of definition of their duties and authority
   B. Tendency of staff personnel almost always to be older than line personnel at comparable salary levels with who they must deal
   C. Selection of staff personnel who fail to have simultaneously both competence in their specialties and skill in staff work
   D. The staff person fails to understand mixed staff and operating duties

9. The one of the following which is the BEST measure of decentralization in an agency is the 9.____
   A. amount of checking required on decisions made at lower levels in the chain of command
   B. amount of checking required on decisions made at lower levels of the chain of command and the number of functions affected thereby
   C. number of functions affected by decisions made at higher levels
   D. number of functions affected by middle echelon decision-making

10. Which of the following is generally NOT a valid statement with respect to the supervisory process? 10.____
   A. General supervision is more effective than close supervision.
   B. Employee-centered supervisors lead more effectively than do production-centered supervisors.
   C. Employee satisfaction is directly related to productivity.
   D. Low-producing supervisors use techniques that are different from high-producing supervisors.

11. The one of the following which is the MOST essential element for proper evaluation of the performance of subordinate supervisors is a 11.____
   A. careful definition of each supervisor's specific job responsibilities and of his progress in meeting mutually agreed upon work goals
   B. system of rewards and penalties based on each supervisor's progress in meeting clearly defined performance standards
   C. definition of personality traits, such as industry, initiative, dependability, and cooperativeness, required for effective job performance
   D. breakdown of each supervisor's job into separate components and a rating of his performance on each individual task

12. The one of the following which is the PRINCIPAL advantage of specialization for the operating efficiency of a public service agency is that specialization 12.____
   A. reduces the amount of red tape in coordinating the activities of mutually dependent departments
   B. simplifies the problem of developing adequate job controls
   C. provides employees with a clear understanding of the relationship of their activities to the overall objectives of the agency
   D. reduces destructive competition for power between departments

13. Of the following, the group which generally benefits MOST from supervisory training programs in public service agencies are those supervisors who have 13.____
   A. accumulated a long period of total service to the agency
   B. responsibility for a large number of subordinate personnel
   C. been in the supervisory ranks for a long period of time
   D. a high level of formalized academic training

14. A list of conditions which encourages good morale inside a work group would NOT include a 14.____
   A. high rate of agreement among group members on values and objectives
   B. tight control system to minimize the risk of individual error
   C. good possibility that joint action will accomplish goals
   D. past history of successful group accomplishment

15. Of the following, the MOST important factor to be considered in selecting a training strategy or program is the 15.____
   A. requirements of the job to be performed by the trainees
   B. educational level or prior training of the trainees
   C. size of the training group
   D. quality and competence of available training specialists

16. Of the following, the one which is considered to be LEAST characteristic of the higher ranks of management is 16.____
    A. that higher levels of management benefit from modern technology
    B. that success is measured by the extent to which objectives are achieved
    C. the number of subordinates that directly report to an executive
    D. the de-emphasis of individual and specialized performance

17. Assume that an executive is preparing a training syllabus to be used in training members of his staff. 17.____
    Which of the following would NOT be a valid principle of the learning process for this manager to keep in mind in the preparation of the training syllabus?
    A. When a person has thoroughly learned a task, it takes a lot of effort to create a little more improvement.
    B. In complicated learning situations, there is a period in which an additional period of practice produces an equal amount of improvement in learning.
    C. The less a person knows about the task, the slower the initial progress.
    D. The more the person knows about the risk, the slower the initial progress.

18. Of the following, which statement BEST illustrates when collective bargaining agreements are working well? 18.____
    A. Executives strongly support subordinate managers.
    B. The management rights clause in the contract is clear and enforced.
    C. Contract provisions are competently interpreted.
    D. The provisions of the agreement are properly interpreted, communicated, and observed.

19. An executive who wishes to encourage subordinates to communicate freely with him about a job-related problem should FIRST 19.____
    A. state his own position on the problem before listening to the subordinates' ideas
    B. invite subordinates to give their own opinions on the problem
    C. ask subordinates for their reactions to his own ideas about the problem
    D. guard the confidentiality of management information about the problem

20. The ability to deal constructively with intra-organizational conflict is an essential attribute of the successful manager. 20.____
    The one of the following types of conflict which would be LEAST difficult to handle constructively is a situation in which there is
    A. agreement on objectives, but disagreement as to the probable results of adopting the various alternatives
    B. agreement on objectives, disagreement on alternative courses of action, and relative certainty as to the outcome of one of the alternatives
    C. disagreement on objectives and on alternate courses of action, but relative certainty as to the outcome of the alternatives
    D. disagreement on objectives and on alternative course of action, but uncertainty as to the outcome of the alternatives

21. Which of the following statements is LEAST accurate in describing formal job evaluation and wage and salary classification plans? 21.____
    A. Parties that disagree on wage matters can examine an established system rather than unsupported opinions.
    B. The use of such plans tends to overlook the effect of age and seniority of employees on job values in the plan.
    C. Such plans can eliminate salary controversies in organizations designing and using them properly.
    D. These plans are not particularly useful in checking on executive compensation.

22. In carrying out disciplinary action, the MOST important procedure for all managers to follow is to 22.____
    A. sell all levels of management on the need for discipline from the organization's viewpoint
    B. follow up on a disciplinary action and not assume that the action has been effective
    C. convince all executives that proper discipline is a legitimate tool for their use
    D. convince all executives that they need to display confidence in the organization's rules

Questions 23-25.

DIRECTIONS: Questions 23 through 25 are to be answered on the basis of the following situation. Richard Ford, a top administrator, is responsible for output in his organization. Because productivity had been lagging for two periods in a row, Ford decided to establish a committee of his subordinate managers to investigate the reasons for the poor performance and to make recommendations for improvements. After two meetings, the committee came to the conclusions and made the recommendations that follow:

Output forecasts had been handed down from the top without prior consultation with middle management and first level supervision. Lines of authority and responsibility had been unclear. The planning and control process should be decentralized.

After receiving the committee's recommendations, Ford proceeded to take the following actions:

Ford decided he would retain final authority to establish quotas but would delegate to the middle managers the responsibility for meeting quotas.

After receiving Ford's decision, the middle managers proceeded to delegate to the first-line supervisors the authority to establish their own quotas. The middle managers eventually received and combined the first-line supervisors' quotas so that these conformed with Ford's.

23. Ford's decision to delegate responsibility for meeting quotas to the middle managers is INCONSISTENT with sound management principles because of which one of the following? 23.____
    A. Ford shouldn't have involved himself in the first place.
    B. Middle managers do not have the necessary skills.

C. Quotas should be established by the chief executive.
D. Responsibility should not be delegated.

24. The principle of co-extensiveness of responsibility and authority bears on Ford's decision. 24.____
In this case, it IMPLIES that
A. authority should exceed responsibility
B. authority should be delegated to match the degree of responsibility
C. both authority and responsibility should be retained and not delegated
D. responsibility should be delegated but authority should be retained

25. The middle manager's decision to delegate to the first-line supervisors the authority to establish quotas was INCORRECTLY reasoned because 25.____
A. delegation and control must go together
B. first-line supervisors are in no position to establish quotas
C. one cannot delegate authority that one does not possess
D. the meeting of quotas should not be delegated

KEY (CORRECT ANSWERS)

1. A
2. C
3. A
4. C
5. C

6. B
7. D
8. B
9. B
10. C

11. A
12. B
13. D
14. B
15. A

16. C
17. D
18. D
19. B
20. B

21. C
22. B
23. D
24. B
25. C

TEST 3

DIRECTIONS: Each question or incomplete statement is followed by several suggested answers or completions. Select the one that BEST answers the question or completes the statement. *PRINT THE LETTER OF THE CORRECT ANSWER IN THE SPACE AT THE RIGHT.*

1. A danger which exists in any organization as complex as that required for administration of a large public agency is that each department comes to believe that it exists for its own sake. 1.____
The one of the following which has been attempted in some organizations as a cure for this condition is to
   A. build up the departmental esprit de corps
   B. expand the functions and jurisdictions of the various departments so that better integration is possible
   C. develop a body of specialists in the various subject matter fields which cut across departmental lines
   D. delegate authority to the lowest possible echelon
   E. systematically transfer administrative personnel from one department to another

2. At best, the organization chart is ordinarily and necessarily an idealized picture of the intent of top management, a reflection of hopes and aims rather than a photograph of the operating facts within the organization. 2.____
The one of the following which is the basic reason for this is that the organization chart
   A. does not show the flow of work within the organization
   B. speaks in terms of positions rather than of live employees
   C. frequently contains unresolved internal ambiguities
   D. is a record of past organization or proposed future organization and never a photograph of the living organization
   E. does not label the jurisdiction assigned to each component unit

3. The drag of inadequacy is always downward. The need in administration is always for the reverse; for a department head to project his thinking to the city level, for the unit chief to try to see the problems of the department. 3.____
The inability of a city administration to recruit administrators who can satisfy this need usually results in departments characterized by
   A. disorganization
   B. poor supervision
   C. circumscribed viewpoints
   D. poor public relations
   E. a lack of programs

4. When, as a result of a shift in public sentiment, the elective officers of a city are changed, is it desirable for career administrators to shift ground without performing any illegal or dishonest act in order to conform to the policies of the new elective officers? 4.____
   A. *No*; the opinions and beliefs of the career officials are the result of long experience in administration and are more reliable than those of politicians

B. *Yes*; only in this way can citizens, political officials, and career administrators alike have confidence in the performance of their respective functions
C. *No*; a top career official who is so spineless as to change his views or procedures as a result of public opinion is of little value to the public service
D. *Yes*; legal or illegal, it is necessary that a city employee carry out the orders of his superior officers
E. *No*; shifting ground with every change in administration will preclude the use of a constant overall policy

5. Participation in developing plans which will affect levels in the organization in addition to his own, will contribute to an individual's understanding of the entire system. When possible, this should be encouraged. 5.____
This policy is, in general,
A. *desirable*; the maintenance of any organization depends upon individual understanding
B. *undesirable*; employees should participate only in these activities which affect their own level, otherwise conflicts in authority may arise
C. *desirable*; an employee's will to contribute to the maintenance of an organization depends to a great extent on the level which he occupies
D. *undesirable*; employees can be trained more efficiently and economically in an organized training program than by participating in plan development
E. *desirable*; it will enable the employee to make intelligent suggestions for adjustment of the plan in the future

6. Constant study should be made of the information contained in reports to isolate those elements of experience which are static, those which are variable and repetitive, and those which are variable and due to chance. 6.____
Knowledge of those elements of experience in his organization which are static or constant will enable the operating official to
A. fix responsibility for their supervisor at a lower level
B. revise the procedure in order to make the elements variable
C. arrange for follow-up and periodic adjustment
D. bring related data together
E. provide a frame of reference within which detailed standards for measurement can be installed

7. A chief staff officer, serving as one of the immediate advisors to the department head, has demonstrated a special capacity for achieving internal agreements and for sound judgment. As a result he has been used more and more as a source of counsel and assistance by the department head. Other staff officers and line officials as well have discovered that it is wise for them to check with this colleague in advance on all problematical matters handed up to the department head. 7.____

Developments such as this are
- A. *undesirable*; they disrupt the normal lines for flow of work in an organization
- B. *desirable*; they allow an organization to make the most of its strength wherever such strength resides
- C. *undesirable*; they tend to undermine the authority of the department head and put it in the hands of a staff officer who does not have the responsibility
- D. *desirable*; they tend to resolve internal ambiguities in organization
- E. *undesirable*; they make for bad morale by causing *cutthroat* competition

8. A common difference among executives is that some are not content unless they are out in front of everything that concerns their organization, while others prefer to run things by pulling strings, by putting others out in front and by stepping into the breach only when necessary. 8.____
Generally speaking, an advantage this latter method of operation has over the former is that it
- A. results in a higher level of morale over a sustained period of time
- B. gets results by exhortation and direct stimulus
- C. makes it unnecessary to calculate integrated moves
- D. makes the personality of the executive felt further down the line
- E. results in the executive getting the reputation for being a good fellow

9. Administrators frequently have to get facts by interviewing people. Although the interview is a legitimate fact gathering technique, it has definite limitations which should not be overlooked. 9.____
The one of the following which is an important limitation is that
- A. people who are interviewed frequently answer questions with guesses rather than admit their ignorance
- B. it is a poor way to discover the general attitude and thinking of supervisors interviewed
- C. people sometimes hesitate to give information during an interview which they will submit in written form
- D. it is a poor way to discover how well employees understand departmental policies
- E. the material obtained from the interview can usually be obtained at lower cost from existing records

10. It is desirable and advantageous to leave a maximum measure of planning responsibility to operating agencies or units, rather than to remove the responsibility to a central planning staff agency. 10.____
Adoption of the former policy (decentralized planning) would lead to
- A. *less effective planning*; operating personnel do not have the time to make long-term plans
- B. *more effective planning*; operating units are usually better equipped technically than any staff agency and consequently are in a better position to set up valid plans
- C. *less effective planning*; a central planning agency has a more objective point of view than any operating agency can achieve

D. *more effective planning*; plans are conceived in terms of the existing situation and their execution is carried out with the will to succeed
E. *less effective planning*; there is little or no opportunity to check deviation from plans in the proposed set-up

Questions 11-15.

DIRECTIONS: The following sections appeared in a report on the work production of two bureaus of a department. Base your answers to Questions 11 through 15 on this information. Throughout the report, assume that each month has 4 weeks.

Each of the two bureaus maintains a chronological file. In Bureau A, every 9 months on the average, this material fills a standard legal size cabinet sufficient for 12,000 work units. In Bureau B the same type of cabinet is filled in 18 months. Each bureau maintains three complete years of information plus a current file. When the current file cabinet is filled, the cabinet containing the oldest material is emptied, the contents disposed of, and the cabinet used for current material. The similarity of these operations makes it possible to consolidate these files with little effort.

Study of the practice of using typists as filing clerks for periods when there is no typing work showed: (1) Bureau A has for the past 6 months completed a total of 1,500 filing work units a week using on the average 100 man-hours of trained file clerk time and 20 man-hours of typist time; (2) Bureau B has in the same period completed a total of 2,000 filing work units a week using on the average 125 man-hours of trained file clerk time and 60 hours of typist time. This includes all work in chronological files. Assuming that all clerks work at the same speed and that all typists work at the same speed, this indicates that work other than filing should be found for typists or that they should be given some training in the filing procedures used. It should be noted that Bureau A has not been producing the 1,600 units of technical (not filing) work per 30-day period required by Schedule K, but is at present 200 units behind. The Bureau should be allowed 3 working days to get on schedule.

11. What percentage (approximate) of the total number of filing work units completed in both units consists of the work involved in the maintenance of the chronological files? 11.____
A. 5% B. 10% C. 15% D. 20% E. 25%

12. If the two chronological files are consolidated, the number of months which should be allowed for filling a cabinet is 12.____
A. 2 B. 4 C. 6 D. 8 E. 14

13. The MAXIMUM number of file cabinets which can be released for other uses as a result of the consolidation recommended is 13.____
A. 0
B. 1
C. 2
D. 3
E. not determinable on the basis of the data given

14. If all the filing work for both units is consolidated without diminution in the amount to be done and all filing work is done by trained file clerks, the number of clerks required (35-hour work week) is 14.____
    A. 4 B. 5 C. 6 D. 7 E. 8

15. In order to comply with the recommendation with respect to Schedule K, the present work production of Bureau A must be increased by 15.____
    A. 50%
    B. 100%
    C. 150%
    D. 200%
    E. an amount which is not determinable

16. A certain training program during World War II resulted in the training of thousands of supervisors in industry. The methods of this program were later successfully applied in various government agencies. The program was based upon the assumption that there is an irreducible minimum of three supervisory skills. 16.____
    The one of these skills among the following is
    A. to know how to perform the job at hand well
    B. to be able to deal personally with workers, especially face-to-face
    C. to be able to imbue workers with the will to perform the job well
    D. to know the kind of work that is done by one's unit and the policies and procedures of one's agency
    E. the *know-how* of administrative and supervisory processes

17. A comment made by an employee about a training course was, "*We never have any idea how we ae getting along in that course.*" 17.____
    The fundamental error in training methods to which this criticism points is
    A. insufficient student participation
    B. failure to develop a feeling of need or active want for the material being presented
    C. the training sessions may be too long
    D. no attempt may have been made to connect the new material with what was already known
    E. no goals have been set for the students

18. Assume that you are attending a departmental conference on efficiency ratings at which it is proposed that a man-to-man rating scale be introduced. 18.____
    You should point out that, of the following, the CHIEF weakness of the man-to-man rating scale is that
    A. it involves abstract numbers rather than concrete employee characteristics
    B. judges are unable to select their own standards for comparison
    C. the standard for comparison shifts from man-to-man for each person rated
    D. not every person rated is given the opportunity to serve as a standard for comparison
    E. standards for comparison will vary from judge to judge

19. Assume that you are conferring with a supervisor who has assigned to his subordinates efficiency ratings which you believe to be generally too low. The supervisor argues that his ratings are generally low because his subordinates are generally inferior. 19.____
Of the following, the evidence MOST relevant to the point at issue can be secured by comparing efficiency ratings assigned by the supervisor
    A. with ratings assigned by other supervisors in the same agency
    B. this year with ratings assigned by him in previous years
    C. to men recently transferred to his unit with ratings previously earned by these men
    D. with the general city average of ratings assigned by all supervisors to all employees
    E. with the relative order of merit of his employees as determined independently by promotion test marks

20. The one of the following which is NOT among the most common of the compensable factors used in wage evaluation studies is 20.____
    A. initiative and ingenuity required
    B. physical demand
    C. responsibility for the safety of others
    D. working conditions
    E. presence of avoidable hazards

21. If independent functions are separated, there is an immediate gain in conserving special skills. If we are to make optimum use of the abilities of our employees, these skills must be conserved. 21.____
Assuming the correctness of this statement, it follows that
    A. if we are not making optimum use of employee abilities, independent functions have not been separated
    B. we are making optimum uses of employee abilities if we conserve special skills
    C. we are making optimum use of employee abilities if independent functions have been separated
    D. we are not making optimum use of employee abilities if we do not conserve special skills
    E. if special skills are being conserved, independent functions need not be separated

22. A reorganization of the bureau to provide for a stenographic pool instead of individual unit stenographers will result in more stenographic help being available to each unit when it is required, and consequently will result in greater productivity for each unit. An analysis of the space requirements shows that setting up a stenographic pool will require a minimum of 400 square feet of good space. In order to obtain this space, it will be necessary to reduce the space available for technical personnel, resulting in lesser productivity for each unit. 22.____

On the basis of the above discussion, it can be stated that, in order to obtain greater productivity for each unit,

A. a stenographic pool should be set up
B. further analysis of the space requirement should be made
C. it is not certain as to whether or not a stenographic pool should be set up
D. the space available for each technician should be increased in order to compensate for the absence of a stenographic pool
E. a stenographic pool should not be set up

23. The adoption of single consolidated form will mean that most of the form will not be used in any one operation. This would create waste and confusion. This conclusion is based upon the unstated hypothesis that 23.____

A. if waste and confusion are to be avoided, a single consolidated form should be used
B. if a single consolidated form is constructed, most of it can be used in each operation
C. if waste and confusion are to be avoided, most of the form employed should be used
D. most of a single consolidation form is not used
E. a single consolidated form should not be used

KEY (CORRECT ANSWERS)

1. E
2. B
3. C
4. B
5. E

6. A
7. B
8. A
9. A
10. D

11. C
12. C
13. B
14. D
15. E

16. B
17. E
18. E
19. C
20. E

21. D
22. C
23. C

PREPARING WRITTEN MATERIAL

PARAGRAPH REARRANGEMENT COMMENTARY

The sentences that follow are in scrambled order. You are to rearrange them in proper order and indicate the letter choice containing the correct answer at the space at the right.

Each group of sentences in this section is actually a paragraph presented in scrambled order. Each sentence in the group has a place in that paragraph; no sentence is to be left out. You are to read each group of sentences and decide upon the best order in which to put the sentences so as to form a well-organized paragraph.

The questions in this section measure the ability to solve a problem when all the facts relevant to its solution are not given.

More specifically, certain positions of responsibility and authority require the employee to discover connection between events sometimes, apparently, unrelated. In order to do this, the employee will find it necessary to correctly infer that unspecified events have probably occurred or are likely to occur. This ability becomes especially important when action must be taken on incomplete information.

Accordingly, these questions require competitors to choose among several suggested alternatives, each of which presents a different sequential arrangement of the events. Competitors must choose the MOST logical of the suggested sequences.

In order to do so, they may be required to draw on general knowledge to infer missing concepts or events that are essential to sequencing the given events. Competitors should be careful to infer only what is essential to the sequence. The plausibility of the wrong alternatives will always require the inclusion of unlikely events or of additional chains of events which are NOT essential to sequencing the given events.

It's very important to remember that you are looking for the best of the four possible choices, and that the best choice of all may not even be one of the answers you're given to choose from.

There is no one right way to solve these problems. Many people have found it helpful to first write out the order of the sentences, as they would have arranged them, on their scrap paper before looking at the possible answers. If their optimum answer is there, this can save them some time. If it isn't, this method can still give insight into solving the problem. Others find it most helpful to just go through each of the possible choices, contrasting each as they go along. You should use whatever method feels comfortable and works for you.

While most of these types of questions are not that difficult, we've added a higher percentage of the difficult type, just to give you more practice. Usually there are only one or two questions on this section that contain such subtle distinctions that you're unable to answer confidently. And you then may find yourself stuck deciding between two possible choices, neither of which you're sure about.

PREPARING WRITTEN MATERIAL

EXAMINATION SECTION

TEST 1

DIRECTIONS: The following groups of sentences need to be arranged in an order that makes sense. Select the letter preceding the sequence that represents the BEST sentence order. *PRINT THE LETTER OF THE CORRECT ANSWER IN THE SPACE AT THE RIGHT.*

1. I. A large Naval station on Alameda Island, near Oakland, held many warships in port, and the War Department was worried that if the bridge were to be blown up by the enemy, passage to and from the bay would be hopelessly blocked. 1.____
II. Though many skeptics were opposed to the idea of building such an enormous bridge, the most vocal opposition came from a surprising source: the United States War Department.
III. The War Department's concerns led to a showdown at San Francisco City Hall between Strauss and the Secretary of War, who demanded to know what would happen if a military enemy blew up the bridge.
IV. In 1933, by submitting a construction cost estimate of $17 million, an engineer named Joseph Strauss won the contract to build the Golden Gate Bridge of San Francisco, which would then become one of the world's largest bridges.
V. Strauss quickly ended the debate by explaining that the Golden Gate Bridge was to be a suspension bridge, whose roadway would hang in the air from cables strung between two huge towers, and would immediately sink into three hundred feet of water if it were destroyed.
The BEST order is:
A. II, III, I, IV, V B. I, II, III, V, IV C. IV, II, I, III, V D. IV, I, III, V, II

2. I. Plastic surgeons have already begun to use virtual reality to map out the complex nerve and tissue structures of a particular patient's face, in order to prepare for delicate surgery. 2.____
II. A virtual reality program responds to these movements by adjusting the images that a person sees on a screen or through goggles, thereby creating an "interactive" world in which a person can see and touch three-dimensional graphic objects.
III. No more than a computer program that is designed to build and display graphic images, the virtual reality program takes graphic programs a step further by sensing a person's head and body movements.
IV. The computer technology known as virtual reality, now in its very first stages of development, is already revolutionizing some aspects of contemporary life.
V. Virtual reality computers are also being used by the space program, most recently to simulate conditions for the astronauts who were launched on a repair mission to the Hubble telescope.

The BEST order is:
A. IV, II, I, V, III B. III, I, V, II, IV C. IV, III, II, I, V D. III, I, II, IV, V

3. I. Before you plant anything, the soil in your plant bed should be carefully raked level, a small section at a time, and any clods or rocks that can't be broken up should be removed. 3.____
II. Your plant should be placed in a hole that will position it at the same level it was at the nursery, and a small indentation should be pressed into the soil around the plant in order to hold water near its roots.
III. Before placing the plant in the soil, lightly separate any roots that may have been matted together in the container, cutting away any thick masses that can't be separated, so that the remaining roots will be able to grow outward.
IV. After the bed is ready, remove your plant from its container by turning it upside down and tapping or pushing on the bottom —never remove it by pulling on the plant.
V. When you bring home a small plant in an individual container from the nursery, there are several things to remember while preparing to plant it in your own garden.

The BEST order is:
A. V, IV, III, II, I B. V, II, IV, III, II C. I, IV, II, III, V D. I, IV, V, II, III

4. I. The motte and its tower were usually built first, so that sentries could use it as a lookout to warn the castle workers of any danger that might approach the castle. 4.____
II. Though the moat and palisade offered the bailey a good deal of protection, it was linked to the motte by a set of stairs that led to a retractable drawbridge at the motte's gate, to enable people to evacuate onto the motte in case of an attack.
III. The motte of these early castles was a fortified hill, sometimes as high as one hundred feet, on which stood a palisade and tower.
IV. The bailey was a clear, level spot below the motte, also enclosed by a palisade, which in turn was surrounded by a large trench or moat.
V. The earliest castles built in Europe were not the magnificent stone giants that still tower over much of the European landscape, but simpler wooden constructions called motte-and-bailey castles.

The BEST order is:
A. V, III, I, IV, II B. V, IV, I, II, III C. I, IV, III, II, V D. I, III, II, IV, V

5. I. If an infant is left alone or abandoned for a short while, its immediate response is to cry loudly, accompanying its screams with aggressive flailing of its legs and limbs. 5.____
II. If a child has been abandoned for a longer period of time, it becomes completely still and quiet, as if realizing that now its only chance for survival is to shut its mouth and remain motionless.
III. Along with their intense fear of the dark, the crying behavior of human infants offers insights into how prehistoric newborn children might have evolved instincts that would prevent them from becoming victims of predators.

IV. This behavior often surprises people who enter a hospital's maternity ward for the first time and encounter total silence from a roomful of infants.
V. This violent screaming response is quite different from an infant's cries of discomfort or hunger, and seems to serve as either the child's first line of defense against an unwanted intruder, or a desperate attempt to communicate its position to the mother.

The BEST order is:
A. III, II, IV, I, V B. III, I, V, II, IV C. I, V, IV, II, III D. II, IV, I, V, III

6. I. When two cats meet who are strangers, their first actions and gestures determine who the "dominant" cat will be, at least for the time being. 6.____
II. Unlike dogs, cats are typically a solitary animal species who avoid social interaction, but they do display specific social responses to each other upon meeting.
III. This is unlikely, however; before such a point of open hostility is reached, one of the cats will usually take the "submissive" position of crouching down while looking away from the other dat.
IV. If a cat desires dominance or sees the other cat as a threat to its territory, it will stare directly at the intruder with a lowered tail.
V. If the other cat responds with a similar gesture, or with the strong defensive posture of an arched back, laid-back ears and raised tail, a fight or chase is likely if neither cat gives in.

The BEST order is:
A. IV, II, I, V, III B. I, II, IV, V, III C. I, IV, V, III, II D. II, I, IV, V, III

7. I. A star or planet's gravitational force can best be explained in this way: anything passing through this "dent" in space will veer toward the star or planet as if it were rolling into a hole. 7.____
II. Objects that are massive or heavy, such as stars or planets, "sink" into this surface, creating a sort of dent or concavity in the surrounding space.
III. Black holes, the most massive objects known to exist in space, create dents so large and deep that the space surrounding them actually folds in on itself, preventing anything that falls in —even light —from ever escaping again.
IV. The sort of dent a star or planet makes depends on how massive it is; planets generally have weak gravitational pulls, but stars, which are larger and heavier, make a bigger "dent" that will attract more matter.
V. In outer space, the force of gravity works as if the surrounding space is a soft, flat surface.

The BEST order is:
A. III, V, II, I, IV B. III, IV, I, V, II C. V, II, I, IV, III D. I, V, II, IV, III

8. I. Eventually, the society of Kyoto gave the world one of its first and greatest novels when Japan's most promising writer, Lady Murasaki Shikibu, wrote her chronicle of Kyoto's society, *The Tale of Genji*, which preceded the first European novels by more than 500 years. 8.____
II. The society of Kyoto was dedicated to the pleasures of art; the courtiers experimented with new and colorful methods of sculpture, painting, writing, decorative gardening, and even making clothes.

III. Japanese culture began under the powerful authority of Chinese Buddhism, which influenced every aspect of Japanese life from religion to politics and art.
IV. This new, vibrant culture was so sophisticated that all the people in Kyoto's imperial court considered themselves poets, and the line between life and art hardly existed —lovers corresponded entirely through written verses, and even government officials communicated by writing poems to each other.
V. In the eighth century, when the emperor established the town of Kyoto as the capital of the Japanese empire, Japanese society began to develop its own distinctive style.

The BEST order is:
A. V, II, IV, I, III B. II, I, V, IV, III C. V, III, IV, I, II D. III, V, II, IV, I

9. I. Instead of wheels, the HSST uses two sets of magnets, one which sits on the track, and another that is carried by the train; these magnets generate an identical magnetic field which forces the two sets apart. 9.____
II. In the last few decades, railway travel has become less popular throughout the world, because it is much slower than travel by airplane, and not much less expensive.
III. The HSST's designers say that the train can take passengers from one town to another as quickly as a jet plane —while consuming less than half the energy.
IV. This repellent effect is strong enough to lift the entire train above the trackway, and the train, literally traveling on air, rockets along at speeds of up to 300 miles per hour.
V. The revolutionary technology of magnetic levitation, currently being tested by Japan's experimental HSST (High Speed Surface Transport), may yet bring passenger trains back from the dead.

The BEST order is:
A. II, V, I, IV, III B. II, I, IV, III, V C. V, II, III, I, IV D. V, I, III, IV, II

10. I. When European countries first began to colonize the African continent, their impression of the African people was of a vast group of loosely organized tribal societies, without any great centralized source of power or wealth. 10.____
II. The legend of Timbuktu persisted until the nineteenth century, when a French adventurer visited Timbuktu and found that raids by neighboring tribesmen had made the city a shadow of its former self.
III. In the fifteenth century, when the stories of travelers who had traveled Africa's Sudan region began circulating around Europe, this impression began to change.
IV. In 1470, an Italian merchant named Benedetto Dei traveled to Timbuktu and confirmed these rumors, describing a thriving metropolis where rich and poor people worshipped together in the city's many ornate mosques — there was even a university in Timbuktu, much like its European counterparts, where African scholars pursued their studies in the arts and sciences.

V. The travelers' legends told of an enormous city in the western Sudan, Timbuktu, where the streets were crowded with goods brought by faraway caravans, and where there was a stone palace as large as any in Europe.

The BEST order is:

A. III, V, I, IV, II B. I, II, IV, III, V C. I, III, V, IV, II D. II, I, III, IV, V

11. I. Also, our reference points in sighting the moon make us believe that its size is changing; when the moon is rising through the trees, it seems huge, because our brains unconsciously compare the size of the moon with the size of the trees in the foreground. 11.____

II. To most people, the sky itself appears more distant at the horizon than directly overhead, and if the moon's size—which remains constant—is projected from the horizon, the apparent distance of the horizon makes the moon look bigger.

III. Up higher in the sky, the moon is set against tiny stars in the background, which will make the moon seem smaller.

IV. People often wonder why the moon becomes bigger when it approaches the horizon, but most scientists agree that this is a complicated optical illusion, produced by at least three factors.

V. The moon illusion may also be partially explained by a phenomenon that has nothing to do with errors in our perception—light that enters the earth's atmosphere is sometimes refracted, and so the atmosphere may act as a kind of magnifying glass for the moon's image.

The BEST order is:

A. IV, III, V, II, I B. IV, II, I, III, V C. V, II, I, III, IV D. II, I, III, IV, V

12. I. When the Native Americans were introduced to the horses used by white explorers, they were amazed at their new alternative—here was an animal that was strong and swift, would patiently carry a person or other loads on its back, and they later discovered, was right at home on the plains. 12.____

II. Before the arrival of European explorers to North America, the natives of the American plains used large dogs to carry their travois-long lodgepoles loaded with clothing, gear, and food.

III. These horses, it is now known, were not really strangers to North America; the very first horses originated here, on this continent, tens of thousands of years ago, and migrated into Asia across the Bering Land Bridge, a strip of land that used to link our continent with the Eastern world.

IV. At first, the natives knew so little about horses that at least one tribe tried to feed their new animals pieces of dried meat and animal fat, and were surprised when the horses turned their heads away and began to eat the grass of the prairie.

V. The American horse eventually became extinct, but its Asian cousins were reintroduced to the New World when the European explorers brought them to live among the Native Americans.

The BEST order is:

A. II, I, IV, III, V B. II, IV, I, III, V C. I, II, IV, III, V D. I, III, V, II, IV

13. I. The dress worn by the dancer is believed to have been adorned in the past by shells which would strike each other as the dancer performed, creating a lovely sound. 13.____
II. Today's jingle-dress is decorated with the tin lids of snuff cans, which are rolled into cones and sewn onto the dress,
III. During the jingle-dress dance, the dancer must blend complicated footwork with a series of gentle hos that cause the cones to jingle in rhythm to a drumbeat.
IV. When contemporary Native American tribes meet for a pow-wow, one of the most popular ceremonies to take place is the women's jingle-dress dance.
V. Besides being more readily available than shells, the lids are thought by many dancers to create a softer, more subtle sound.
The BEST order is:
A. II, IV, V, I, III B. IV, II, I, III, V C. II, I, III, V, IV D. IV, I, II, V, III

14. I. If a homeowner lives where seasonal climates are extreme, deciduous shade trees—which will drop their leaves in the winter and allow sunlight to pass through the windows—should be planted near the southern exposure in order to keep the house cool during the summer. 14.____
II. This trajectory is shorter and lower in the sky than at any other time of year during the winter, when a house most requires heating; the northern-facing parts of a house do not receive any direct sunlight at all.
III. In designing an energy-efficient house, especially in colder climates, it is important to remember that most of the house's windows should face south.
IV. Though the sun always rises in the east and sets in the west, the sun of the northern hemisphere is permanently situated in the southern portion of the sky.
V. The explanation for why so many architects and builders want this "southern exposure" is related to the path of the sun in the sky.
The BEST order is:
A. III, I, V, IV, II B. III, V, IV, II, I C. I, III, IV, II, V D. I, II, V, IV, III

15. I. His journeying lasted twenty-four years and took him over an estimated 75,000 miles, a distance that would not be surpassed by anyone other than Magellan—who sailed around the world—for another six hundred years. 15.____
II. Perhaps the most far-flung of these lesser-known travelers was Ibn Batuta, an African Moslem who left his birthplace of Tangier in the summer of 1325.
III. Ibn Batuta traveled all over Africa and Asia, from Niger to Peking, and to the islands of Maldive and Indonesia.
IV. However, a few explorers of the Eastern world logged enough miles and adventures to make Marco Polo's voyage look like an evening stroll.
V. In America, the most well-known of the Old World's explorers are usually Europeans such as Marco Polo, the Italian who brought many elements of Chinese culture to the Western world.
The BEST order is:
A. V, IV, II, III, I B. V, IV, III, II, I C. III, II, I, IV, V D. II, III, I, IV, V

16. I. In the rainforests of South America, a rare species of frog practices a reproductive method that is entirely different from this standard process. 16.____
II. She will eventually carry each of the tadpoles up into the canopy and drop each into its own little pool, where it will be easy to locate and safe from most predators.
III. After fertilization, the female of the species, who lives almost entirely on the forest floor, lays between 2 and 16 eggs among the leaf litter at the base of a tree, and stands watch over these eggs until they hatch.
IV. Most frogs are pond-dwellers who are able to deposit hundreds of eggs in the water and then leave them alone, knowing that enough eggs have been laid to insure the survival of some of their offspring.
V. Once the tadpoles emerge, the female backs in among them, and a tadpole will wriggle onto her back to be carried high into the forest canopy, where the female will deposit it in a little pool of water cupped in the leaf of a plant.
The BEST order is:
A. I, IV, III, II, V B. I, III, V, II, IV C. IV, III, II, V, I D. IV, I, III, V, II

17. I. Eratosthenes had heard from travelers that at exactly noon on June 21, in the ancient city of Aswan, Egypt, the sun cast no shadow in a well, which meant that the sun must be directly overhead. 17.____
II. He knew the sun always cast a shadow in Alexandria, and so he figured that if he could measure the length of an Alexandria shadow at the time when there was no shadow in Aswan, he could calculate the angle of the sun, and therefore the circumference of the earth.
III. The evidence for a round earth was not new in 1492; in fact, Eratosthenes, an Alexandrian geographer who lived nearly sixteen centuries before Columbus's voyage (275-195 B.C.), actually developed a method for calculating the circumference of the earth that is still in use today.
IV. Eratosthenes's method was correct, but his result—28,700 miles—was about 15 percent too high, probably because of the inaccurate ancient methods of keeping time, and because Aswan was not due south of Alexandria, as Eratosthenes had believed.
V. When Christopher Columbus sailed across the Atlantic Ocean for the first time in 1492, there were still some people in the world who ignored scientific evidence and believed that the earth was flat, rather than round.
The BEST order is:
A. I, II, V, III, IV B. V, III, IV, I, II C. V, III, I, II, IV D. III, V, I, II, IV

18. I. The first name for the child is considered a trial naming, often impersonal and neutral, such as the Ngoni name *Chabwera*, meaning "it has arrived." 18.____
II. This sort of name is not due to any parental indifference to the child, but is a kind of silent recognition of Africa's sometimes high infant death rate; most parents ease the pain of losing a child with the belief that it is not really a person until it has been given a final name.
III. In many tribal African societies, families often give two different names to their children, at different periods in time.
IV. After the trial naming period has subsided and it is clear that the child will survive, the parents choose a final name for the child, an act that symbolically completes the act of birth.

V. In fact, some African first-given names are explicitly uncomplimentary, translating as "I am dead" or "I am ugly," in order to avoid the jealousy of ancestral spirits who might wish to take a child that is especially healthy or attractive.

The BEST order is:

A. III, I, II, V, IV B. III, IV, II, I, V C. IV, III, I, II, V D. IV, V, III, I, II

19. I. Though uncertain of the definite reasons for this behavior, scientists believe the birds digest the clay in order to counteract toxins contained in the seeds of certain fruits that are eaten by macaws. 19.____

II. For example, all macaws flock to riverbanks at certain times of the year to eat the clay that is found in river mud.

III. The macaws of South America are not only among the largest and most beautifully colored of the world's flying birds, but they are also one of the smartest.

IV. It is believed that macaws are forced to resort to these toxic fruits during the dry season, when foods are more scarce.

V. The macaw's intelligence has led to intense study by scientists, who have discovered some macaw behaviors that have not yet been explained.

The BEST order is:

A. III, IV, I, II, V B. III, V, II, I, IV C. V, II, I, IV, III D. IV, I, II, III, V

20. I. Although Maggie Kuhn has since passed away, the Gray Panthers are still waging a campaign to reinstate the historical view of the elderly as people whose experience allows them to make their greatest contribution in their later years. 20.____

II. In 1972, an elderly woman named Maggie Kuhn responded to this sort of treatment by forming a group called the Gray Panthers, an organization of both old and young adults with the common goal of creating change.

III. This attitude is reflected strongly in the way elderly people are treated by our society; many are forced into early retirement, or are placed in rest homes in which they are isolated from their communities.

IV. Unlike most other cultures around the world, Americans tend to look upon old age with a sense of dread and sadness.

V. Kuhn believed that when the elderly are forced to withdraw into lives that lack purpose, society loses one of its greatest resources: people who have a lifetime of experience and wisdom to offer their communities.

The BEST order is:

A. IV, III, II, V, I B. IV, II, I, III, V C. II, IV, III, V, I D. II, I, IV, III, V

21. I. The current theory among most anthropologists is that humans evolved from apes who lived in trees near the grasslands of Africa. 21.____

II. Still, some anthropologists insist that such an invention was necessary for the survival of early humans, and point to the Kung Bushmen of central Africa as a society in which the sling is still used in this way.

III. Two of these inventions—fire, and weapons such as spears and clubs—were obvious defenses against predators, and there is archaeological evidence to support the theory of their use.

IV. Once people had evolved enough to leave the safety of trees and walk upright, they needed the protection of several inventions in order to survive.
V. But another invention, a feather or fiber sling that allowed mothers to carry children while leaving their hands free to gather roots or berries, would certainly have decomposed and left behind no trace of itself.

The BEST order is:
A. I, II, III, V, IV B. IV, I, II, III, V C. I, IV, III, V, II D. IV, III, V, II, I

22. I. The person holding the bird should keep it in hot water up to its neck, and the person cleaning should work a mild solution of dishwashing liquid into the bird's plumage, paying close attention to the head and neck. 22.____
II. When rinsing the bird, after all the oil has been removed, the running water should be directed against the lay of its feathers, until water begins to bead off the surface of the feathers—a sign that all the detergent has been rinsed out.
III. If you have rescued a sea bird from an oil spill and want to restore it to clean and normal living, you need a large sink, a constant supply of running hot water (a little over 100ºF), and regular dishwashing liquid.
IV. This cleaning with detergent solution should be repeated as many times as it takes to remove all traces of oil from the bird's feathers, sometime over a period of several days.
V. But before you begin to clean the bird, you must find a partner because cleaning an oiled bird is a two-person job.

The BEST order is:
A. III, I, II, IV, V B. III, V, I, IV, II C. III, I, IV, V, II D. III, IV, V, I, II

23. I. The most difficult time of year for the Tsaatang is the spring calving, when the reindeer leave their wintering ground and rush to their accustomed calving place, without stopping by night or by day. 23.____
II. Reindeer travel in herds, and though some animals are tamed by the Tsaatang for riding or milking, the herds are allowed to roam free.
III. This journey is hard for the Tsaatang, who carry all their possessions with them, but once it's over it proves worthwhile; the Tsaatang can immediately begin to gather milk from reindeer cows who have given birth.
IV. The Tsaatang, a small tribe who live in the far northwest corner of Mongolia, practice a lifestyle that is completely dependent on the reindeer, their main resource for food, clothing, and transport.
V. The people must follow their yearly migrations, living in portable shelters that resemble Native American tepees.

The BEST order is:
A. I, III, II, V, IV B. I, IV, II, V, III C. IV, I, III, V, II D. IV II, V, I, III

24. I. The Romans later improved this system by installing these heated pipe networks throughout walls and ceilings, supplying heat to even the uppermost floors of a building—a system that, to this day, hasn't been much improved. 24.____
II. Air-conditioning, the method by which humans control indoor temperatures, was practiced much earlier than most people think.

III. The earliest heating devices other than open fires were used in 350 B.C. by the ancient Greeks, who directed air that had been heated by underground fires into baked clay pipes that ran under the floor.

IV. Ironically, the first successful cooling system, patented in England in 1831, used fire as its main energy source—fires were lit in the attic of a building, creating an updraft of air that drew cool air into the building through ducts that had underground openings near the river Thames.

V. Cooling buildings was more of a challenge, and wasn't attempted until 1500: a water-based system, designed by Leonardo da Vinci, does not appear to have been successful, since it was never used again.

The BEST order is:

A. III, V, IV, I, II B. III, I, II, V, IV C. II, III, I, V, IV D. IV, II, III, I, V

25. I. Cold, dry air from Canada passes over the Rocky Mountains and sweeps down onto the plains, where it collides with warm, moist air from the waters of the Gulf of Mexico, and when the two air masses meet, the resulting disturbance sometimes forms a violent funnel cloud that strikes the earth and destroys virtually everything in its path. 25.____

II. Hurricanes, storms which are generally not this violent and last much longer, are usually given names by meteorologists, but this tradition cannot be applied to tornados, which have a life span measured in minutes and disappear in the same way as they are born—unnamed.

III. A tornado funnel forms rotating columns of air whose speed reaches three hundred miles an hour—a speed that can only be estimated, because no wind-measuring devices in the direct path of a storm have ever survived.

IV. The natural phenomena known as tornados occur primarily over the Midwestern grasslands of the United States.

V. It is here, meteorologists tell us, that conditions for the formation of tornados are sometimes perfect during the spring months.

The BEST order is:

A. II IV, V, I, III B. II, III, I, V, IV C. IV, V, I, III, II D. IV, III, I, V, II

KEY (CORRECT ANSWERS)

1.	C	11.	B
2.	C	12.	A
3.	B	13.	D
4.	A	14.	B
5.	B	15.	A
6.	D	16.	D
7.	C	17.	C
8.	D	18.	A
9.	A	19.	B
10.	C	20.	A

21.	C
22.	B
23.	D
24.	C
25.	C

EXAMINATION SECTION

TEST 1

DIRECTIONS: The sentences that follow are in scrambled order. You are to rearrange them in proper order and indicate the letter choice containing the correct answer. *PRINT THE LETTER OF THE CORRECT ANSWER IN THE SPACE AT THE RIGHT.*

1. Below are four statements labeled W, X, Y and Z. 1.____
   W. He was a strict and fanatic drillmaster.
   X. The word is always used in a derogatory sense and generally shows resentment and anger on the part of the user.
   Y. It is from the name of this Frenchman that we derive our English word, martinet.
   Z. Jean Martinet was the Inspector-General of Infantry during the reign of King Louis XIV.

   The PROPER order in which these sentences should be placed in a paragraph is:
   A. X, Z, W, Y B. X, Z, Y, W C. Z, W, Y, X D. Z, Y, W, X

2. In the following paragraph, the sentences, which are numbered, have been jumbled. 2.____
   I. Since then it has undergone changes.
   II. It was incorporated in 1955 under the laws of the State of New York.
   III. Its primary purposes, a cleaner city, has, however, remained the same.
   IV. The Citizens Committee works in cooperation with the Mayor's Inter-departmental Committee for a Clean City. 3.____

   The order in which these sentences should be arranged to form a well-organized paragraph is:
   A. II, IV, I, III B. III, IV, I, II C. IV, II, I, III D. IV, III, II, I

Questions 3-5.

DIRECTIONS: The sentences listed below are part of a meaningful paragraph but they are not given in their proper order. You are to decide what would be the BEST order in which to put the sentences so as to form a well-organized paragraph. Each sentence has a place in the paragraph; there are no extra sentences. You are then to answer Questions 3 through 5 inclusive on the basis of your rearrangements of these scrambled sentences into a properly organized paragraph.

In 1887 some insurance companies organized an Inspection Department to advise their clients on all phases of fire prevention and protection. Probably this has been due to the smaller annual fire losses in Great Britain than in the United States. It tests various fire prevention devices and appliances and determines manufacturing hazards and their safeguards. Fire research began earlier in the United States and is more advanced than in Great Britain. Later they established a laboratory specializing in electrical, mechanical, hydraulic, and chemical fields.

3. When the five sentences are arranged in proper order, the paragraph starts with the sentence which begins 3.____
   A. "In 1887..." B. "Probably this..." C. "It tests..."
   D. "Fire research..." E. "Later they..."

4. In the last sentence listed above, "they" refers to 4.____
   A. the insurance companies B. the United States and Great Britain
   C. the Inspection Department D. clients
   E. technicians

5. When the above paragraph is properly arranged, it ends with the words 5.____
   A. "...and protection." B. "...the United States."
   C. "...their safeguards." D. "...in Great Britain."
   E. "...chemical fields."

KEY (CORRECT ANSWERS)

1. C
2. C
3. D
4. A
5. C

TEST 2

DIRECTIONS: In each of the questions numbered I through V, several sentences are given. For each question, choose as your answer the group of number that represents the MOST logical order of these sentences if they were arranged in paragraph form. *PRINT THE LETTER OF THE CORRECT ANSWER IN THE SPACE AT THE RIGHT.*

1. I. It is established when one shows that the landlord has prevented the tenant's enjoyment of his interest in the property leased. 1.____
   II. Constructive eviction is the result of a breach of the covenant of quiet enjoyment implied in all leases.
   III. In some parts of the United States, it is not complete until the tenant vacates within a reasonable time.
   IV. Generally, the acts must be of such serious and permanent character as to deny the tenant the enjoyment of his possessing rights.
   V. In this event, upon abandonment of the premises, the tenant's liability for that ceases.

   The CORRECT answer is:
   A. II, I, IV, III, V
   B. V, II, III, I, IV
   C. IV, III, I, II, V
   D. I, III, V, IV, II

2. I. The powerlessness before private and public authorities that is the typical experience of the slum tenant is reminiscent of the situation of blue-collar workers all through the nineteenth century. 2.____
   II. Similarly, in recent years, this chapter of history has been reopened by anti-poverty groups which have attempted to organize slum tenants to enable them to bargain collectively with their landlords about the conditions of their tenancies.
   III. It is familiar history that many of the worker remedied their condition by joining together and presenting their demands collectively.
   IV. Like the workers, tenants are forced by the conditions of modern life into substantial dependence on these who possess great political aid and economic power.
   V. What's more, the very fact of dependence coupled with an absence of education and self-confidence makes them hesitant and unable to stand up for what they need from those in power.

   The CORRECT answer is:
   A. V, IV, I, II, III
   B. II, III, I, V, IV
   C. III, I, V, IV, II
   D. I, IV, V, III, II

3. I. A railroad, for example, when not acting as a common carrier may contract away responsibility for its own negligence. 3.____
   II. As to a landlord, however, no decision has been found relating to the legal effect of a clause shifting the statutory duty of repair to the tenant.
   III. The courts have not passed on the validity of clauses relieving the landlord of this duty and liability.
   IV. They have, however, upheld the validity of exculpatory clauses in other types of contracts.

V. Housing regulations impose a duty upon the landlord to maintain leased premises in safe condition.
VI. As another example, a bailee may limit his liability except for gross negligence, willful acts, or fraud.

The CORRECT answer is:
A. II, I, VI, IV, III, V
B. I, III, IV, V, VI, II
C. III, V, I, IV, II, VI
D. V, III, IV, I, VI, II

4. I. Since there are only samples in the building, retail or consumer sales are generally eschewed by mart occupants, and in some instances, rigid controls are maintained to limit entrance to the mart only to those persons engaged in retailing. 4.____
II. Since World War I, in many larger cities, there has developed a new type of property, called the mart building.
III. It can, therefore, be used by wholesalers and jobbers for the display of sample merchandise.
IV. This type of building is most frequently a multi-storied, finished interior property which is a cross between a retail arcade and a loft building.
V. This limitation enables the mart occupants to ship the orders from another location after the retailer or dealer makes his selection from the samples.

The CORRECT answer is:
A. II, IV, III, I, V
B. IV, III, V, I, II
C. I, III, II, IV, V
D. I, IV, II, III, V

5. I. In general, staff-line friction reduces the distinctive contribution of staff personnel. 5.____
II. The conflicts, however, introduce an uncontrolled element into the managerial system.
III. On the other hand, the natural resistance of the line to staff innovations probably usefully restrains over-eager efforts to apply untested procedures on a large scale.
IV. Under such conditions, it is difficult to know when valuable ideas are being sacrificed.
V. The relatively weak position of staff, requiring accommodation to the line, tends to restrict their ability to engage in free, experimental innovation.

The CORRECT answer is:
A. IV, II, III, I, V
B. I, V, III, II, IV
C. V, III, I, II, IV
D. II, I, IV, V, III

KEY (CORRECT ANSWERS)

1. A
2. D
3. D
4. A
5. B

TEST 3

DIRECTIONS: Questions 1 through 4 consist of six sentences which can be arranged in a logical sequence. For each question, select the choice which places the numbered sentences in the MOST logical sequent. *PRINT THE LETTER OF THE CORRECT ANSWER IN THE SPACE AT THE RIGHT.*

1. I. The burden of proof as to each issue is determined before trial and remains upon the same party throughout the trial. 1.____
   II. The jury is at liberty to believe one witness' testimony as against a number of contradictory witnesses.
   III. In a civil case, the party bearing the burden of proof is required to prove his contention by a fair preponderance of the evidence.
   IV. However, it must be noted that a fair preponderance of evidence does not necessarily mean a greater number of witnesses.
   V. The burden of proof is the burden which rests upon one of the parties to an action to persuade the trier of the facts, generally the jury, that a proposition he asserts is true.
   VI. If the evidence is equally balanced, or if it leaves the jury in such doubt as to be unable to decide the controversy either way, judgment must be given against the party upon whom the burden of proof rests.

   The CORRECT answer is:
   A. III, II, V, IV, I, VI
   B. I, II, VI, V, III, IV
   C. III, IV, V, I, II, VI
   D. V, I, III, VI, IV, II

2. I. If a parent is without assets and is unemployed, he cannot be convicted of the crime of non-support of a child. 2.____
   II. The term "sufficient ability" has been held to mean sufficient financial ability.
   III. It does not matter if his unemployment is by choice or unavoidable circumstances.
   IV. If he fails to take any steps at all, he may be liable to prosecution for endangering the welfare of a child.
   V. Under the penal law, a parent is responsible for the support of his minor child only if the parent is "of sufficient ability."
   VI. An indigent parent may meet his obligation by borrowing money or by seeking aid under the provisions of the Social Welfare Law.

   The CORRECT answer is:
   A. VI, I, V, III, II, IV
   B. I, III, V, II, IV, VI
   C. V, II, I, III, VI, IV
   D. I, VI, IV, V, II, III

3. I. Consider, for example, the case of a rabble rouser who urges a group of twenty people to go out and break the windows of a nearby factory. 3.____
   II. Therefore, the law fills the indicated gap with the crime of inciting to riot.
   III. A person is considered guilty of inciting to riot when he urges ten or more persons to engage in tumultuous and violent conduct of a kind likely to create public alarm.
   IV. However, if he has not obtained the cooperation of at least four people, he cannot be charged with unlawful assembly.

V. The charge of inciting to riot was added to the law to cover types of conduct which cannot be classified as either the crime of "riot" or the crime of "unlawful assembly."
VI. If he acquires the acquiescence of at least four of them, he is guilty of unlawful assembly even if the project does not materialize.

The CORRECT answer is:

A. III, V, I, VI, IV, II
B. V, I, IV, VI, II, III
C. III, IV, I, V, II, VI
D. V, I, IV, VI, III, II

4. I. If, however, the rebuttal evidence presents an issue of credibility, it is for the jury to determine whether the presumption has, in fact, been destroyed. 4.____
II. Once sufficient evidence to the contrary is introduced, the presumption disappears from the trial.
III. The effect of a presumption is to place the burden upon the adversary to come forward with evidence to rebut the presumption.
IV. When a presumption is overcome and ceases to exist in the case, the fact or facts which gave rise to the presumption still remain.
V. Whether a presumption has been overcome is ordinarily a question for the court.
VI. Such information may furnish a basis for a logical inference.

The CORRECT answer is:

A. IV, VI, II, V, I, III
B. III, II, V, I, IV, VI
C. V, III, VI, IV, II, I
D. V, IV, I, II, VI, III

KEY (CORRECT ANSWERS)

1. D
2. C
3. A
4. B

PREPARING WRITTEN MATERIALS

EXAMINATION SECTION

TEST 1

DIRECTIONS: Each question contains a sentence. Read each sentence carefully to decide whether it is correct. Then, in the space at the right, mark your answer:

A. If the sentence is incorrect because of bad grammar or sentence structure;
B. If the sentence is incorrect because of bad punctuation
C. If the sentence is incorrect because of bad capitalization
D. If the sentence is correct.

Each incorrect sentence has only one type of error. Consider a sentence correct if it has no errors, although there may be other correct ways of saying the same thing.

SAMPLE QUESTION i: One of our clerks were promoted yesterday.

The subject of this sentence is *one*, so the verb should be *was promoted* instead of *were promoted*. Since the sentence is incorrect because of bad grammar, the answer to Sample Question I is A.

SAMPLE QUESTION II: Between you and me, I would prefer not going there.

Since this sentence is correct, the answer to Sample Question II is D.

1. The National alliance of Businessmen is trying to persuade private businesses to hire youth in the summertime. 1.____

2. The supervisor who is on vacation, is in charge of processing vouchers. 2.____

3. The activity of the committee at its conferences is always stimulating. 3.____

4. After checking the addresses again, the letters went to the mailroom. 4.____

5. The director, as well as the employees, are interested in sharing the dividends. 5.____

6. The experiments conducted by professor Alford were described at a recent meeting of our organization. 6.____

7. I shall be glad to discuss these matters with whoever represents the Municipal Credit Union. 7.____

8. In my opinion, neither Mr. Price nor Mr. Roth knows how to operate this office appliance. 8.____

9. The supervisor, as well as the other stenographers, were unable to transcribe Miss Johnson's shorthand notes. 9.____

10. Important functions such as, recruiting and training, are performed by our unit. 10.____

11. Realizing that many students are interested in this position, we sent announcements to all the High Schools. 11.____

12. After pointing out certain incorrect conclusions, the report was revised by Mr. Clark and submitted to Mr. Batson. 12.____

13. The employer contributed two hundred dollars; the employees, one hundred dollars. 13.____

14. He realized that the time, when a supervisor could hire and fire, was over. 14.____

15. The complaints received by Commissioner Regan was the cause of the change in policy. 15.____

16. Any report, that is to be sent to the Federal Security Administration, must be approved and signed by Mr. Yound. 16.____

17. Of the two stenographers, Miss Rand is the more accurate. 17.____

18. Since the golf courses are crowded during the summer, more men are needed to maintain the courses in good playing condition. 18.____

19. Although he invited Mr. Frankel and I to attend a meeting of the Civil Service Assembly, we were unable to accept his invitation. 19.____

20. Only the employees who worked overtime last week may leave one hour earlier today. 20.____

21. We need someone who can speak french fluently. 21.____

22. A tall, elderly, man entered the office and asked to see Mr. Brown. 22.____

23. The clerk insisted that he had filed the correspondence in the proper cabinet. 23.____

24. "Will you assist us," he asked? 24.____

25. According to the information contained in the report, a large quantity of paper and envelopes were used by this bureau last year. 25.____

KEY (CORRECT ANSWERS)

1.	C	11.	C
2.	B	12.	A
3.	D	13.	D
4.	A	14.	B
5.	A	15.	A
6.	C	16.	B
7.	D	17.	D
8.	D	18.	C
9.	A	19.	A
10.	B	20.	D

21. C
22. B
23. D
24. B
25. A

TEST 2

DIRECTIONS: Each question consists of a sentence which may be classified appropriately under one of the following four categories:

A. Incorrect because of faulty grammar or sentence structure.
B. Incorrect because of faulty punctuation.
C. Incorrect because of faulty capitalization.
D. Correct

Examine each sentence carefully. Then, in the space at the right, print the capital letter preceding the option which is the BEST of the four suggested above. All incorrect sentences contain only one type of error. Consider a sentence correct if it contains none of the types of errors mentioned, although there may be other correct ways of expressing the same thought.

1. Mrs. Black the supervisor of the unit, has many important duties. 1.____

2. We spoke to the man whom you saw yesterday. 2.____

3. When a holiday falls on sunday, it is officially celebrated on monday. 3.____

4. Of the two reports submitted, this one is the best. 4.____

5. Each staff member, including the accountants, were invited to the meeting. 5.____

6. Give the package to whomever calls for it. 6.____

7. To plan the work is our responsibility; to carry it out is his. 7.____

8. "May I see the person in charge of this office," asked the visitor? 8.____

9. He knows that it was not us who prepared the report. 9.____

10. These problems were brought to the attention of senator Johnson. 10.____

11. The librarian classifies all books periodicals and documents. 11.____

12. Any employee who uses an adding machine realizes its importance. 12.____

13. Instead of coming to the office, the clerk should of come to the supply room. 13.____

14. He asked, "will your staff assist us?" 14.____

15. Having been posted on the bulletin board, we were certain that the announcements would be read. 15.____

16. He was not informed, that he would have to work overtime. 16.____

17. The wind blew several paper off of his desk. 17.____

18. Charles Dole, who is a member of the committee, was asked to confer with commissioner Wilson. 18.____

19. Miss Bell will issue a copy to whomever asks for one. 19.____

20. Most employees, and he is no exception do not like to work overtime. 20.____

21. This is the man whom you interviewed last week. 21.____

22. Of the two cities visited, White Plains is the cleanest. 22.____

23. Although he was willing to work on other holidays, he refused to work on Labor day. 23.____

24. If an employee wishes to attend the conference, he should fill out the necessary forms. 24.____

25. The division chief reports that an engineer and an inspector is needed for this special survey. 25.____

KEY (CORRECT ANSWERS)

1. B
2. D
3. C
4. A
5. A

6. A
7. D
8. B
9. A
10. C

11. B
12. D
13. A
14. C
15. A

16. B
17. A
18. C
19. A
20. B

21. D
22. A
23. C
24. D
25. A

TEST 3

DIRECTIONS: Each question consists of a sentence which may be classified appropriately under one of the following four categories:

A. Incorrect because of faulty grammar or sentence structure.
B. Incorrect because of faulty punctuation.
C. Incorrect because of faulty capitalization.
D. Correct

Examine each sentence carefully. Then, in the space at the right, print the capital letter preceding the option which is the BEST of the four suggested above. All incorrect sentences contain only one type of error. Consider a sentence correct if it contains none of the types of errors mentioned, although there may be other correct ways of expressing the same thought.

1. We have learned that there was more than twelve people present at the meeting. 1.____

2. Every one of the employees is able to do this kind of work. 2.____

3. Neither the supervisor nor his assistant are in the office today. 3.____

4. The office manager announced that any clerk, who volunteered for the assignment, would be rewarded. 4.____

5. After looking carefully in all the files, the letter was finally found on a desk. 5.____

6. In answer to the clerk's question, the supervisor said, "this assignment must be completed today." 6.____

7. The office manager says that he can permit only you and me to go to the meeting. 7.____

8. The supervisor refused to state who he would assign to the reception unit. 8.____

9. At the last meeting, he said that he would interview us in september. 9.____

10. Mr. Jones, who is one of our most experienced employees has been placed in charge of the main office. 10.____

11. I think that this adding machine is the most useful of the two we have in our office. 11.____

12. Between you and I, our new stenographer is not as competent as our former stenographer. 12.____

13. The new assignment should be given to whoever can do the work rapidly 13.____

14. Mrs. Smith, as well as three other typists, was assigned to the new office. 14.____

15. The staff assembled for the conference on time but, the main speaker arrived late. 15.____

16. The work was assigned to Miss Green and me. 16.____

17. The staff regulations state that an employee, who is frequently tardy, may receive a negative evaluation. 17.____

18. He is the kind of person who is always willing to undertake difficult assignments. 18.____

19. Mr. Wright's request cannot be granted under no conditions. 19.____

20. George Colt a new employee, was asked to deliver the report to the Domestic Relations Court. 20.____

21. The supervisor entered the room and said, "The work must be completed today." 21.____

22. The employees were given their assignments and, they were asked to begin work immediately. 22.____

23. The letter will be sent to the United States senate this week. 23.____

24. When the supervisor entered the room, he noticed that the book was laying on the desk. 24.____

25. The price of the pens were higher than the price of the pencils. 25.____

KEY (CORRECT ANSWERS)

1.	A	11.	A
2.	D	12.	A
3.	A	13.	D
4.	B	14.	D
5.	A	15.	B
6.	C	16.	D
7.	D	17.	B
8.	A	18.	D
9.	C	19.	A
10.	B	20.	B

21.	D
22.	B
23.	C
24.	A
25.	A

PREPARING WRITTEN MATERIAL

EXAMINATION SECTION

TEST 1

DIRECTIONS: Each question consists of a sentence which may or may not be an example of good English usage. Examine each sentence, considering grammar, punctuation, spelling, capitalization, and awkwardness. Then choose the correct statement about it from the four choices below it. If the English usage in the sentence given is better than any of the changes suggested in choices B, C, or D, pick choice A. (Do not pick a choice that will change the meaning of the sentence.) *PRINT THE LETTER OF THE CORRECT ANSWER IN THE SPACE AT THE RIGHT.*

1. We attended a staff conference on Wednesday the new safety and fire rules were discussed. 1.____
   A. This is an example of acceptable writing.
   B. The words "safety," "fire," and "rules" should begin with capital letters.
   C. There should be a comma after the word "Wednesday."
   D. There should be a period after the word "Wednesday" and the word "the" should begin with a capital letter.

2. Neither the dictionary or the telephone directory could be found in the office library. 2.____
   A. This is an example of acceptable writing.
   B. The word "or" should be changed to "nor."
   C. The word "library" should be spelled "libery."
   D. The word "neither" should be changed to "either."

3. The report would have been typed correctly if the typist could read the draft. 3.____
   A. This is an example of acceptable writing.
   B. The word "would" should be removed.
   C. The word "have" should be inserted after the word "could."
   D. The word "correctly" should be changed to "correct."

4. The supervisor brought the reports and forms to an employees desk. 4.____
   A. This is an example of acceptable writing.
   B. The word "brought" should be changed to "took."
   C. There should be a comma after the word "reports" and a comma after the word "forms."
   D. The word "employees" should be spelled "employee's."

5. It's important for all the office personnel to submit their vacation schedules on time. 5.____
   A. This is an example of acceptable writing.
   B. The word "It's" should be spelled "Its."
   C. The word "their" should be spelled "they're."
   D. The word "personnel" should be spelled "personal."

6. The report, along with the accompanying documents, were submitted for review. 6.____
   A. This is an example of acceptable writing.
   B. The words "were submitted" should be changed to "was submitted."
   C. The word "accompanying" should be spelled "accompaning."
   D. The comma after the word "report" should be taken out.

7. If others must use your files, be certain that they understand how the system works, but insist that you do all the filing and refiling. 7.____
   A. This is an example of acceptable writing.
   B. There should be a period after the word "works," and the word "but" should start a new sentence.
   C. The words "filing" and "refiling" should be spelled "fileing" and "refileing."
   D. There should be a comma after the word "but."

8. The appeal was not considered because of its late arrival. 8.____
   A. This is an example of acceptable writing.
   B. The word "its" should be changed to "it's."
   C. The word "its" should be changed to "the."
   D. The words "late arrival" should be changed to "arrival late."

9. The letter must be read carefuly to determine under which subject it should be filed. 9.____
   A. This is an example of acceptable writing.
   B. The word "under" should be changed to "at."
   C. The word "determine" should be spelled "determin."
   D. The word "carefuly" should be spelled "carefully."

10. He showed potential as an office manager, but he lacked skill in delegating work. 10.____
   A. This is an example of acceptable writing.
   B. The word "delegating" should be spelled "delagating."
   C. The word "potential" should be spelled "potencial."
   D. The words "he lacked" should be changed to "was lacking."

KEY (CORRECT ANSWERS)

1.	D	6.	B
2.	B	7.	A
3.	C	8.	A
4.	D	9.	D
5.	A	10.	A

TEST 2

DIRECTIONS: Each question consists of a sentence which may or may not be an example of good English usage. Examine each sentence, considering grammar, punctuation, spelling, capitalization, and awkwardness. Then choose the correct statement about it from the four choices below it. If the English usage in the sentence given is better than any of the changes suggested in choices B, C, or D, pick choice A. (Do not pick a choice that will change the meaning of the sentence.) *PRINT THE LETTER OF THE CORRECT ANSWER IN THE SPACE AT THE RIGHT.*

1. The supervisor wants that all staff members report to the office at 9:00 A.M. 1.____
   A. This is an example of acceptable writing.
   B. The word "that" should be removed and the word "to" should be inserted after the word "members."
   C. There should be a comma after the word "wants" and a comma after the word "office."
   D. The word "wants" should be changed to "want" and the word "shall" should be inserted after the word "members."

2. Every morning the clerk opens the office mail and distributes it. 2.____
   A. This is an example of acceptable writing.
   B. The word "opens" should be changed to "open."
   C. The word "mail" should be changed to "letters."
   D. The word "it" should be changed to "them."

3. The secretary typed more fast on a desktop computer than on a laptop computer. 3.____
   A. This is an example of acceptable writing.
   B. The words "more fast" should be changed to "faster."
   C. There should be a comma after the words "desktop computer."
   D. The word "than" should be changed to "then."

4. The new stenographer needed a desk a computer, a chair and a blotter. 4.____
   A. This is an example of acceptable writing.
   B. The word "blotter" should be spelled "blodder."
   C. The word "stenographer" should begin with a capital letter.
   D. There should be a comma after the word "desk."

5. The recruiting officer said, "There are many different goverment jobs available." 5.____
   A. This is an example of acceptable writing.
   B. The word "There" should not be capitalized.
   C. The word "government" should be spelled "government."
   D. The comma after the word "said" should be removed.

6. He can recommend a mechanic whose work is reliable. 6.____
   A. This is an example of acceptable writing.
   B. The word "reliable" should be spelled "relyable."
   C. The word "whose" should be spelled "who's."
   D. The word "mechanic should be spelled "mecanic."

7. She typed quickly; like someone who had not a moment to lose. 7.____
   A. This is an example of acceptable writing.
   B. The word "not" should be removed.
   C. The semicolon should be changed to a comma.
   D. The word "quickly" should be placed before instead of after the word "typed."

8. She insisted that she had to much work to do. 8.____
   A. This is an example of acceptable writing.
   B. The word "insisted" should be spelled "incisted."
   C. The word "to" used in front of "much" should be spelled "too."
   D. The word "do" should be changed to "be done."

9. He excepted praise from his supervisor for a job well done. 9.____
   A. This is an example of acceptable writing.
   B. The word "excepted" should be spelled "accepted."
   C. The order of the words "well done" should be changed to "done well."
   D. There should be a comma after the word "supervisor."

10. What appears to be intentional errors in grammar occur several times in the passage. 10.____
   A. This is an example of acceptable writing.
   B. The word "occur" should be spelled "occurr."
   C. The word "appears" should be changed to "appear."
   D. The phrase "several times" should be changed to "from time to time."

KEY (CORRECT ANSWERS)

1.	B	6.	A
2.	A	7.	C
3.	B	8.	C
4.	D	9.	B
5.	C	10.	C

TEST 3

DIRECTIONS: Each question consists of a sentence which may or may not be an example of good English usage. Examine each sentence, considering grammar, punctuation, spelling, capitalization, and awkwardness. Then choose the correct statement about it from the four choices below it. If the English usage in the sentence given is better than any of the changes suggested in choices B, C, or D, pick choice A. (Do not pick a choice that will change the meaning of the sentence.) *PRINT THE LETTER OF THE CORRECT ANSWER IN THE SPACE AT THE RIGHT.*

1. The clerk could have completed the assignment on time if he knows where these materials were located. 1.____
   A. This is an example of acceptable writing.
   B. The word "knows" should be replaced by "had known."
   C. The word "were" should be replaced by "had been."
   D. The words "where these materials were located" should be replaced by "the location of these materials."

2. All employees should be given safety training. Not just those who accidents. 2.____
   A. This is an example of acceptable writing.
   B. The period after the word "training" should be changed to a colon.
   C. The period after the word "training" should be changed to a semicolon, and the first letter of the word "Not" should be changed to a small "n."
   D. The period after the word "training" should be changed to a comma, and the first letter of the word "Not" should be changed to a small "n."

3. This proposal is designed to promote employee awareness of the suggestion program, to encourage employee participation in the program, and to increase the number of suggestions submitted. 3.____
   A. This is an example of acceptable writing.
   B. The word "proposal" should be spelled "proposal."
   C. The words "to increase the number of suggestions submitted" should be changed to "an increase in the number of suggestions is expected."
   D. The word "promote" should be changed to "enhance" and the word "increase" should be changed to "add to."

4. The introduction of inovative managerial techniques should be preceded by careful analysis of the specific circumstances and conditions in each department. 4.____
   A. This is an example of acceptable writing.
   B. The word "technique" should be spelled "techneques."
   C. The word "inovative" should be spelled "innovative."
   D. A comma should be placed after the word "circumstances" and after the word "conditions."

5. This occurrence indicates that such criticism embarrasses him. 5.____
   A. This is an example of acceptable writing.
   B. The word “occurrence” should be spelled “occurence.”
   C. The word “criticism” should be spelled “critisism.
   D. The word “embarrasses” should be spelled “embarasses.

KEY (CORRECT ANSWERS)

1. B
2. D
3. A
4. C
5. A

EXAMINATION SECTION

TEST 1

DIRECTIONS: Each question or incomplete statement is followed by several suggested answers or completions. Select the one that BEST answers the question or completes the statement. *PRINT THE LETTER OF THE CORRECT ANSWER IN THE SPACE AT THE RIGHT.*

1. When conducting a needs assessment for the purpose of education planning, an agency's FIRST step is to identify or provide 1.____
   A. a profile of population characteristics
   B. barriers to participation
   C. existing resources
   D. profiles of competing resources

2. Research has demonstrated that of the following, the MOST effective medium for communicating with external publics is(are) 2.____
   A. video news releases
   B. television
   C. radio
   D. newspapers

3. Basic ideas behind the effort to influence the attitudes and behaviors of a constituency include each of the following EXCEPT the idea that 3.____
   A. words, rather than actions or events, are most likely to motivate
   B. demands for action are a usual response
   C. self-interest usually figures heavily into public involvement
   D. the reliability of change programs is difficult to assess

4. An agency representative is trying to craft a pithy message to constituents in order to encourage the use of agency program resources.
   Choosing an audience for such messages is easiest when the message 4.____
   A. is project- or behavior-based
   B. is combined with other messages
   C. is abstract
   D. has a broad appeal

5. Of the following factors, the MOST important to the success of an agency's external education or communication programs is the 5.____
   A. amount of resources used to implement them
   B. public's prior experiences with the agency
   C. real value of the program to the public
   D. commitment of the internal audience

6. A representative for a state agency is being interviewed by a reporter from a local news network. The representative is being asked to defend a program that is extremely unpopular in certain parts of the municipality.
   When a constituency is known to be opposed to a position, the MOST useful communication strategy is to present 6.____

A. only the arguments that are consistent with constituents' views
B. only the agency's side of the issue
C. both sides of the argument as clearly as possible
D. both sides of the argument, omitting key information about the opposing position

7. The MOST significant barriers to effective agency community relations include 7.____
I. widespread distrust of communication strategies
II. the media's "watchdog" stance
III. public apathy
IV. statutory opposition

The CORRECT answer is:
A. I only B. I and II C. II and III D. III and IV

8. In conducting an education program, many agencies use workshops and seminars in a classroom setting. 8.____
Advantages of classroom-style teaching over other means of educating the public include each of the following, EXCEPT
A. enabling an instructor to verify learning through testing and interaction with the target audience
B. enabling hands-on practice and other participatory learning techniques
C. ability to reach an unlimited number of participants in a given length of time
D. ability to convey the latest, most up-to-date information

9. The _____ model of community relations is characterized by an attempt to persuade the public to adopt the agency's point of view. 9.____
A. two-way symmetric B. two-way asymmetric
C. public information D. press agency/publicity

10. Important elements of an internal situation analysis include the 10.____
I. list of agency opponents II. communication audit
III. updated organizational almanac IV. stakeholder analysis

The CORRECT answer is:
A. I and II B. I, II, and III C. II and III D. I, II, III and IV

11. Government agency information efforts typically involve each of the following objectives, EXCEPT to 11.____
A. implement changes in the policies of government agencies to align with public opinion
B. communicate the work of agencies
C. explain agency techniques in a way that invites input from citizens
D. provide citizen feedback to government administrators

12. Factors that are likely to influence the effectiveness of an educational campaign include the 12.____
    I. level of homogeneity among intended participants
    II. number and types of media used
    III. receptivity of the intended participants
    IV. level of specificity in the message or behavior to be taught

    The CORRECT answer is:
    A. I and II B. I, II, and III C. II and III D. I, II, III, and IV

13. An agency representative is writing instructional objectives that will later help to measure the effectiveness of an educational program. 13.____
    Which of the following verbs, included in an objective, would be MOST helpful for the purpose of measuring effectiveness?
    A. Know B. Identify C. Learn D. Comprehend

14. A state education agency wants to encourage participation in a program that has just received a boost through new federal legislation. The program is intended to include participants from a wide variety of socioeconomic and other demographic characteristics. The agency wants to launch a broad-based program that will inform virtually every interested party in the state about the program's new circumstances. 14.____
    In attempting to deliver this message to such a wide-ranging constituency, the agency's BEST practice would be to
    A. broadcast the same message through as many different media channels as possible
    B. focus on one discrete segment of the public at a time
    C. craft a message whose appeal is as broad as the public itself
    D. let the program's achievements speak for themselves and rely on word-of-mouth

15. Advantages associated with using the World Wide Web as an educational tool include 15.____
    I. an appeal to younger generations of the public
    II. visually-oriented, interactive learning
    III. learning that is not confined by space, time, or institutional association
    IV. a variety of methods for verifying use and learning

    The CORRECT answer is:
    A. I only B. I and II C. I, II, and III D. I, II, II, and IV

16. In agencies involved in health care, community relations is a critical function because it 16.____
    A. serves as an intermediary between the agency and consumers
    B. generates a clear mission statement for agency goals and priorities
    C. ensures patient privacy while satisfying the media's right to information
    D. helps marketing professionals determine the wants and needs of agency constituents

17. After an extensive campaign to promote its newest program to constituents, an agency learns that most of the audience did not understand the intended message. 17.____
MOST likely, the agency has
   A. chosen words that were intended to inform, rather than persuade
   B. not accurately interpreted what the audience really needed to know
   C. overestimated the ability of the audience to receive and process the message
   D. compensated for noise that may have interrupted the message

18. The necessary elements that lead to conviction and motivation in the minds of participants in an educational or information program include each of the following, EXCEPT the _____ of the message. 18.____
   A. acceptability
   B. intensity
   C. single-channel appeal
   D. pervasiveness

19. Printed materials are often at the core of educational programs provided by public agencies. 19.____
The PRIMARY disadvantage associated with print is that it
   A. does not enable comprehensive treatment of a topic
   B. is generally unreliable in term of assessing results
   C. is often the most expensive medium available
   D. is constrained by time

20. Traditional thinking on public opinion holds that there is about _____ percent of the public who are pivotal to shifting the balance and momentum of opinion—they are concerned about an issue, but not fanatical, and interested enough to pay attention to a reasoned discussion. 20.____
   A. 2
   B. 10
   C. 33
   D. 51

21. One of the most useful guidelines for influencing attitude change among people is to 21.____
   A. invite the target audience to come to you, rather than approaching them
   B. use moral appeals as the primary approach
   C. use concrete images to enable people to see the results of behaviors or indifference
   D. offer tangible rewards to people for changes in behavior

22. An agency is attempting to evaluate the effectiveness of its educational program. For this purpose, it wants to observe several focus groups discussing the same program. 22.____
Which of the following would NOT be a guideline for the use of focus groups?
   A. Focus groups should only include those who have participated in the program.
   B. Be sure to accurately record the discussion.
   C. The same questions should be asked at each focus group meeting.
   D. It is often helpful to have a neutral, non-agency employee facilitate discussions.

23. Research consistently shows that _____ is the determinant most likely to make a newspaper editor run a news release. 23.____
    A. novelty B. prominence C. proximity D. conflict

24. Which of the following is NOT one of the major variables to take into account when considering a population-needs assessment? 24.____
    A. State of program development
    B. Resources available
    C. Demographics
    D. Community attitudes

25. The FIRST step in any communications audit is to 25.____
    A. develop a research instrument
    B. determine how the organization currently communicates
    C. hire a contractor
    D. determine which audience to assess

KEY (CORRECT ANSWERS)

1.	A	11.	A
2.	D	12.	D
3.	A	13.	B
4.	A	14.	B
5.	D	15.	C
6.	C	16.	A
7.	D	17.	B
8.	C	18.	C
9.	B	19.	B
10.	C	20.	B

21.	C
22.	A
23.	C
24.	C
25.	D

TEST 2

DIRECTIONS: Each question or incomplete statement is followed by several suggested answers or completions. Select the one that BEST answers the question or completes the statement. *PRINT THE LETTER OF THE CORRECT ANSWER IN THE SPACE AT THE RIGHT.*

1. A public relations practitioner at an agency has just composed a press release highlighting a program's recent accomplishments and success stories. 1.____
In pitching such releases to print outlets, the practitioner should
I. e-mail, mail, or send them by messenger
II. address them to "editor" or "news director"
III. have an assistant call all media contacts by telephone
IV. ask reporters or editors how they prefer to receive them

The CORRECT answer is:
A. I and II B. I and IV C. II, III, and IV D. III only

2. The "output goals" of an educational program are MOST likely to include 2.____
A. specified ratings of services by participants on a standardized scale
B. observable effects on a given community or clientele
C. the number of instructional hours provided
D. the number of participants served

3. An agency wants to evaluate satisfaction levels among program participants, and mails out questionnaires to everyone who has been enrolled in the last year. 3.___
The PRIMARY problem associated with this method of evaluative research is that it
A. poses a significant inconvenience for respondents
B. is inordinately expensive
C. does not allow for follow-up or clarification questions
D. usually involves a low response rate

4. A communications audit is an important tool for measuring 4.____
A. the depth of penetration of a particular message or program
B. the cost of the organization's information campaigns
C. how key audiences perceive an organization
D. the commitment of internal stakeholders

5. The "ABCs" of written learning objectives include each of the following, EXCEPT 5.____
A. Audience B. Behavior C. Conditions D. Delineation

6. When attempting to change the behaviors of constituents, it is important to keep in mind that 6.____
   I. most people are skeptical of communications that try to get them to change their behaviors
   II. in most cases, a person selects the media to which he exposes himself
   III. people tend to react defensively to messages or programs that rely on fear as a motivating factor
   IV. programs should aim for the broadest appeal possible in order to include as many participants as possible

   The CORRECT answer is:
   A. I and II B. I, II and III C. II and III D. I, II, III, and IV

7. The "laws" of public opinion include the idea that it is 7.____
   A. useful for anticipating emergencies
   B. not sensitive to important events
   C. basically determined by self-interest
   D. sustainable through persistent appeals

8. Which of the following types of evaluations is used to measure public attitudes before and after an information/educational program? 8.____
   A. Retrieval study B. Copy test
   C. Quota sampling D. Benchmark study

9. The PRIMARY source for internal communications is(are) usually 9.____
   A. flow charts B. meetings
   C. voice mail D. printed publications

10. An agency representative is putting together informational materials—brochures and a newsletter—outlining changes in one of the state's biggest benefits programs. 10.____
    In assembling print materials as a medium for delivering information to the public, the representative should keep in mind each of the following trends:
    I. For various reasons, the reading capabilities of the public are in general decline
    II. Without tables and graphs to help illustrate the changes, it is unlikely that the message will be delivered effectively
    III. Professionals and career-oriented people are highly receptive to information written in the form of a journal article or empirical study
    IV. People tend to be put off by print materials that use itemized and bulleted (●) lists

    The CORRECT answer is:
    A. I and II B. I, II and III C. II and III D. I, II, III, and IV

11. Which of the following steps in a problem-oriented information campaign would typically be implemented FIRST? 11.____
    A. Deciding on tactics
    B. Determining a communications strategy
    C. Evaluating the problem's impact
    D. Developing an organizational strategy

12. A common pitfall in conducting an educational program is to 12.____
    A. aim it at the wrong target audience
    B. overfund it
    C. leave it in the hands of people who are in the business of education, rather than those with expertise in the business of the organization
    D. ignore the possibility that some other organization is meeting the same educational need for the target audience

13. The key factors that affect the credibility of an agency's educational program include 13.____
    A. organization
    B. scope
    C. sophistication
    D. penetration

14. Research on public opinion consistently demonstrates that it is 14.____
    A. easy to move people toward a strong opinion on anything, as long as they are approached directly through their emotions
    B. easier to move people away from an opinion they currently hold than to have them form an opinion about something they have not previously cared about
    C. easy to move people toward a strong opinion on anything, as long as the message appeals to their reason and intellect
    D. difficult to move people toward a strong opinion on anything, no matter what the approach

15. In conducting an education program, many agencies use meetings and conferences to educate an audience about the organization and its programs. Advantages associated with this approach include 15.____
    I. a captive audience that is known to be interested in the topic
    II. ample opportunities for verifying learning
    III. cost-efficient meeting space
    IV. the ability to provide information on a wider variety of subjects

    The CORRECT answer is:
    A. I and II
    B. I, III and IV
    C. II and III
    D. I, II, III and IV

16. An agency is attempting to evaluate the effectiveness of its educational programs. For this purpose, it wants to observe several focus groups discussing particular programs. 16.____
    For this purpose, a focus group should never number more than _____ participants.
    A. 5
    B. 10
    C. 15
    D. 20

17. A _____ speech is written so that several agency members can deliver it to different audiences with only minor variations. 17._____
    A. basic B. printed C. quota D. pattern

18. Which of the following statements about public opinion is generally considered to be FALSE? 18._____
    A. Opinion is primarily reactive rather than proactive.
    B. People have more opinions about goals than about the means by which to achieve them.
    C. Facts tend to shift opinion in the accepted direction when opinion is not solidly structured.
    D. Public opinion is based more on information than desire.

19. An agency is trying to promote its educational program. 19._____
    As a general rule, the agency should NOT assume that
    A. people will only participate if they perceive an individual benefit
    B. promotions need to be aimed at small, discrete groups
    C. if the program is good, the audience will find out about it
    D. a variety of methods, including advertising, special events, and direct mail, should be considered

20. In planning a successful educational program, probably the first and most important question for an agency to ask is: 20._____
    A. What will be the content of the program?
    B. Who will be served by the program?
    C. When is the best time to schedule the program?
    D. Why is the program necessary?

21. Media kits are LEAST likely to contain 21._____
    A. fact sheets B. memoranda
    C. photographs with captions D. news releases

22. The use of pamphlets and booklets as media for communication with the public often involves the disadvantage that 22._____
    A. the messages contained within them are frequently nonspecific
    B. it is difficult to measure their effectiveness in delivering the message
    C. there are few opportunities for people to refer to them
    D. color reproduction is poor

23. The MOST important prerequisite of a good educational program is an 23._____
    A. abundance of resources to implement it
    B. individual staff unit formed for the purpose of program delivery
    C. accurate needs assessment
    D. uneducated constituency

24. After an education program has been delivered, an agency conducts a program evaluation to determine whether its objectives have been met. 24.____
General rules about how to conduct such an education program valuation include each of the following, EXCEPT that it
    A. must be done immediately after the program has been implemented
    B. should be simple and easy to use
    C. should be designed so that tabulation of responses can take place quickly and inexpensively
    D. should solicit mostly subjective, open-ended responses if the audience was large

25. Using electronic media such as television as means of educating the public is typically recommended ONLY for agencies that 25.____
    I. have a fairly simple message to begin with
    II. want to reach the masses, rather than a targeted audience
    III. have substantial financial resources
    IV. accept that they will not be able to measure the results of the campaign with much precision

The CORRECT answer is:
A. I and II B. I, II and III C. II and IV D. I, II, III and IV

KEY (CORRECT ANSWERS)

1. B
2. C
3. D
4. C
5. D

6. B
7. C
8. D
9. D
10. A

11. C
12. D
13. A
14. D
15. B

16. B
17. D
18. D
19. C
20. D

21. B
22. B
23. C
24. D
25. D

PRINCIPLES AND PRACTICES, OF ADMINISTRATION, SUPERVISION AND MANAGEMENT

TABLE OF CONTENTS

PRINCIPLES AND PRACTICES, OF ADMINISTRATION, SUPERVISION AND MANAGEMENT

Most people are inclined to think of administration as something that only a few persons are responsible for in a large organization. Perhaps this is true if you are thinking of Administration with a capital *A*, but administration with a lower case *a* is a responsibility of supervisors at all levels each working day.

All of us feel we are pretty good supervisors and that we do a good job of administering the workings of our agency. By and large, this is true, but every so often it is good to check up on ourselves. Checklists appear from time to time in various publications which psychologists say tell whether or not a person will make a good wife, husband, doctor, lawyer, or supervisor.

The following questions are an excellent checklist to test yourself as a supervisor and administrator.

Remember, Administration gives direction and points the way but administration carries the ideas to fruition. Each is dependent on the other for its success. Remember, too, that no unit is too small for these departmental functions to be carried out. These statements apply equally as well to the Chief Librarian as to the Department Head with but one or two persons to supervise.

GENERAL ADMINISTRATION: General Responsibilities of Supervisors

1. Have I prepared written statements of functions, activities, and duties for my organizational unit?

2. Have I prepared procedural guides for operating activities?

3. Have I established clearly in writing, lines of authority and responsibility for my organizational unit?

4. Do I make recommendations for improvements in organization, policies, administrative and operating routines and procedures, including simplification of work and elimination of non-essential operations?

5. Have I designated and trained an understudy to function in my absence?

6. Do I supervise and train personnel within the unit to effectively perform their assignments?

7. Do I assign personnel and distribute work on such a basis as to carry out the organizational unit's assignment or mission in the most effective and efficient manner?

8. Have I established administrative controls by:

    a. Fixing responsibility and accountability on all supervisors under my direction for the proper performance of their functions and duties.

b. Preparations and submitting periodic work load and progress reports covering the operations of the unit to my immediate superior.

c. Analysis and evaluation of such reports received from subordinate units.

d. Submission of significant developments and problems arising within the organizational unit to my immediate superior.

e. Conducting conferences, inspections, etc., as to the status and efficiency of unit operations.

9. Do I maintain an adequate and competent working force?

10. Have I fostered good employee-department relations, seeing that established rules, regulations, and instructions are being carried out properly?

11. Do I collaborate and consult with other organizational units performing related functions to insure harmonious and efficient working relationships?

12. Do I maintain liaison through prescribed channels with city departments and other governmental agencies concerned with the activities of the unit?

13. Do I maintain contact with and keep abreast of the latest developments and techniques of administration (professional societies, groups, periodicals, etc.) as to their applicability to the activities of the unit?

14. Do I communicate with superiors and subordinates through prescribed organizational channels?

15. Do I notify superiors and subordinates in instances where bypassing is necessary as soon thereafter as practicable?

16. Do I keep my superior informed of significant developments and problems?

SEVEN BASIC FUNCTIONS OF THE SUPERVISOR

I. PLANNING

This means working out goals and means to obtain goals. What needs to be done, who will do it, how, when, and where it is to be done.

SEVEN STEPS IN PLANNING

A. Define job or problem clearly.
B. Consider priority of job.
C. Consider time-limit—starting and completing.
D. Consider minimum distraction to, or interference with, other activities.
E. Consider and provide for contingencies—possible emergencies.
F. Break job down into components.

G. Consider the 5 W's and H:
   WHY..........is it necessary to do the job? (Is the purpose clearly defined?)
   WHAT........needs to be done to accomplish the defined purpose?
   ....is needed to do the job? (Money, materials, etc.)
   WHO..........is needed to do the job?
   ....will have responsibilities?
   WHERE......is the work to be done?
   WHEN........is the job to begin and end? (Schedules, etc.)
   HOW..........is the job to bed done? (Methods, controls, records, etc.)

II. ORGANIZING

This means dividing up the work, establishing clear lines of responsibility and authority and coordinating efforts to get the job done.

III. STAFFING

The whole personnel function of bringing in and training staff, getting the right man and fitting him to the right job—the job to which he is best suited.

In the normal situation, the supervisor's responsibility regarding staffing normally includes providing accurate job descriptions, that is, duties of the jobs, requirements, education and experience, skills, physical, etc.; assigning the work for maximum use of skills; and proper utilization of the probationary period to weed out unsatisfactory employees.

IV. DIRECTING

Providing the necessary leadership to the group supervised. Important work gets done to the supervisor's satisfaction.

V. COORDINATING

The all-important duty of inter-relating the various parts of the work.
The supervisor is also responsible for controlling the coordinated activities. This means measuring performance according to a time schedule and setting quotas to see that the goals previously set are being reached. Reports from workers should be analyzed, evaluated, and made part of all future plans.

VI. REPORTING

This means proper and effective communication to your superiors, subordinates, and your peers (in definition of the job of the supervisor). Reports should be read and information contained therein should be used, not be filed away and forgotten. Reports should be written in such a way that the desired action recommended by the report is forthcoming.

VII. BUDGETING
This means controlling current costs and forecasting future costs. This forecast is based on past experience, future plans and programs, as well as current costs.

You will note that these seven functions can fall under three topics:

Planning) Organizing) Make a plan	Staffing) Directing) Get things done Controlling)	Reporting) Budgeting) Watch it work

PLANNING TO MEET MANAGEMENT GOALS

I. WHAT IS PLANNING?

A. Thinking a job through before new work is done to determine the best way to do it
B. A method of doing something
C. Ways and means for achieving set goals
D. A means of enabling a supervisor to deliver with a minimum of effort, all details involved in coordinating his work

II. WHO SHOULD MAKE PLANS?

Everybody!
All levels of supervision must plan work. (Top management, heads of divisions or bureaus, first line supervisors, and individual employees.) The higher the level, the more planning required.

III. WHAT ARE THE RESULTS OF POOR PLANNING?

A. Failure to meet deadline
B. Low employee morale
C. Lack of job coordination
D. Overtime is frequently necessary
E. Excessive cost, waste of material and manhours

IV. PRINCIPLES OF PLANNING

A. Getting a clear picture of your objectives. What exactly are you trying to accomplish?
B. Plan the whole job, then the parts, in proper sequence.
C. Delegate the planning of details to those responsible for executing them.
D. Make your plan flexible.
E. Coordinate your plan with the plans of others so that the work may be processed with a minimum of delay.
F. Sell your plan before you execute it.
G. Sell your plan to your superior, subordinate, in order to gain maximum participation and coordination.
H. Your plan should take precedence. Use knowledge and skills that others have brought to a similar job.
I. Your plan should take account of future contingencies; allow for future expansion.
J. Plans should include minor details. Leave nothing to chance that can be anticipated.
K. Your plan should be simple and provide standards and controls. Establish quality and quantity standards and set a standard method of doing the job. The controls will indicate whether the job is proceeding according to plan.
L. Consider possible bottlenecks, breakdowns, or other difficulties that are likely to arise.

V. Q. WHAT ARE THE YARDSTICKS BY WHICH PLANNING SHOULD BE MEASURED?
A. Any plan should:
- —Clearly state a definite course of action to be followed and goal to be achieved, with consideration for emergencies.
- — Be realistic and practical.
- — State what's to be done, when it's to be done, where, how, and by whom.
- — Establish the most efficient sequence of operating steps so that more is accomplished in less time, with the least effort, and with the best quality results.
- — Assure meeting deliveries without delays.
- — Establish the standard by which performance is to be judged.

Q. WHAT KINDS OF PLANS DOES EFFECTIVE SUPERVISION REQUIRE?
A. Plans should cover such factors as:
- — Manpower: right number of properly trained employees on the job
- — Materials: adequate supply of the right materials and supplies
- — Machines: full utilization of machines and equipment, with proper maintenance
- — Methods: most efficient handling of operations
- — Deliveries: making deliveries on time
- — Tools: sufficient well-conditioned tools
- — Layout: most effective use of space
- — Reports: maintaining proper records and reports
- — Supervision: planning work for employees and organizing supervisor's own time

MANAGEMENT PRINCIPLES

I. MANAGEMENT
Q. What do we mean by management?
A. Getting work done through others.

Management could also be defined as planning, directing, and controlling the operations of a bureau or division so that all factors will function properly and all persons cooperate efficiently for a common objective.

II. MANAGEMENT PRINCIPLES

A. There should be a hierarchy—wherein authority and responsibility run upward and downward through several levels—with a broad base at the bottom and a single head at the top.

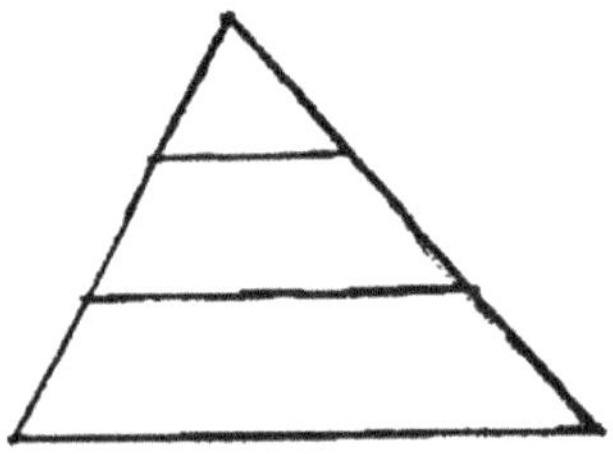

B. Each and every unit or person in the organization should be answerable ultimately to the manager at the apex. In other words, *The buck stops here!*

C. Every necessary function involved in the bureau's objectives is assigned to a unit in that bureau.

D. Responsibilities assigned to a unit are specifically clear-cut and understood.

E. Consistent methods of organizational structure should be applied at each level of the organization.

F. Each member of the bureau from top to bottom knows: to whom he reports and who reports to him.

G. No member of one bureau reports to more than one supervisor. No dual functions.

H. Responsibility for a function is matched by authority necessary to perform that function. Weight of authority.

I. Individuals or units reporting to a supervisor do not exceed the number which can be feasibly and effectively coordinated and directed. Concept of *span of control.*

J. Channels of command (management) are not violated by staff units, although there should be staff services to facilitate and coordinate management functions.

K. Authority and responsibility should be decentralized to units and individuals who are responsible for the actual performance of operations.
Welfare – down to Welfare Centers
Hospitals – down to local hospitals

L. Management should exercise control through attention to policy problems of exceptional performance, rather than through review of routine actions of subordinates.

M. Organizations should never be permitted to grow so elaborate as to hinder work accomplishments.

III. ORGANIZATION STRUCTURE

Types of Organizations
The purest form is a leader and a few followers, such as:

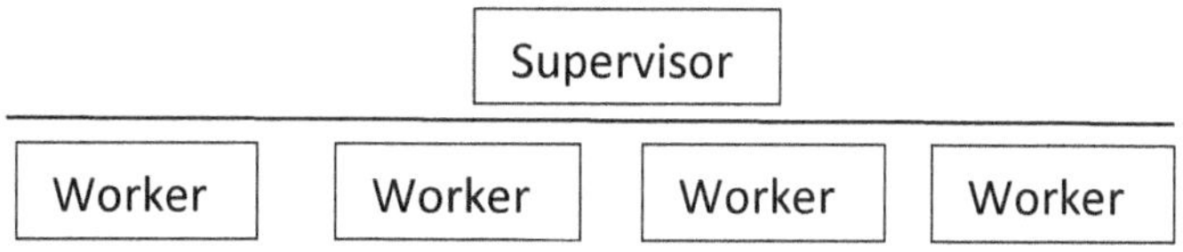

(Refer to organization chart) from supervisor to workers.

The line of authority is direct, The workers know exactly where they stand in relation to their boss, to whom they report for instructions and direction.

Unfortunately, in our present complex society, few organizations are similar to this example of a pure line organization. In this era of specialization, other people are often needed in the simplest of organizations. These specialists are known as staff. The sole purpose for their existence (staff) is to assist, advise, suggest, help or counsel line organizations. Staff has no authority to direct line people—nor do they give them direct instructions.

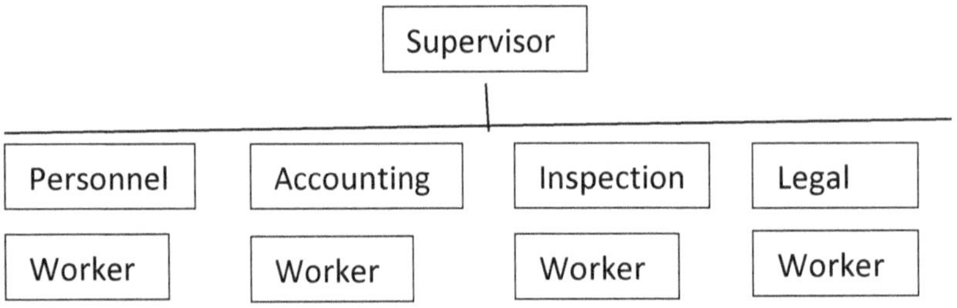

Line Functions
1. Directs
2. Orders
3. Responsibility for carrying out activities from beginning to end
4. Follows chain of command
5. Is identified with what it does
6. Decides when and how to use staff advice
7. Line executes

Staff Functions
1. Advises
2. Persuades and sells
3. Staff studies, reports, recommends but does not carry out
4. May advise across department lines
5. May find its ideas identified with others
6. Has to persuade line to want its advice
7. Staff: Conducts studies and research. Provides advice and instructions in technical matters. Serves as technical specialist to render specific services.

Types and Functions of Organization Charts

An organization chart is a picture of the arrangement and inter-relationship of the subdivisions of an organization.

A. Types of Charts:
   1. Structural: basic relationships only
   2. Functional: includes functions or duties
   3. Personnel: positions, salaries, status, etc.
   4. Process Chart: work performed
   5. Gantt Chart: actual performance against planned
   5. Flow Chart: flow and distribution of work

B. Functions of Charts:
   1. Assist in management planning and control
   2. Indicate duplication of functions
   3. Indicate incorrect stressing of functions
   4. Indicate neglect of important functions
   5. Correct unclear authority
   6. Establish proper span of control

C. Limitations of Charts:
   1. Seldom maintained on current basis
   2. Chart is oversimplified
   3. Human factors cannot adequately be charted

D. Organization Charts should be:
   1. Simple
   2. Symmetrical
   3. Indicate authority
   4. Line and staff relationship differentiated
   5. Chart should be dated and bear signature of approving officer
   6. Chart should be displayed, not hidden

ORGANIZATION

There are four basic principles of organization:
1. Unity of command
2. Span of control
3. Uniformity of assignment
4. Assignment of responsibility and delegation of authority

I. UNITY OF COMMAND

Unity of command means that each person in the organization should receive orders from one, and only one, supervisor. When a person has to take orders from two or more people, (a) the orders may be in conflict and the employee is upset because he does not know which he should obey, or (b) different orders may reach him at the same time and he does not know which he should carry out first.

Equally as bad as having two bosses is the situation where the supervisor is bypassed. Let us suppose you are a supervisor whose boss bypasses you (deals directly with people reporting to you). To the worker, it is the same as having two bosses; but to you, the supervisor, it is equally serious. Bypassing on the part of your boss will undermine your authority, and the people under you will begin looking to your boss for decisions and even for routine orders.

You can prevent bypassing by telling the people you supervise that if anyone tries to give them orders, they should direct that person to you.

II. SPAN OF CONTROL

Span of control on a given level involves:
A. The number of people being supervised
B. The distance
C The time involved in supervising the people. (One supervisor cannot supervise too many workers effectively.)

Span of control means that a supervisor has the right number (not too many and not too few) of subordinates that he can supervise well.

III. UNIFORMITY OF ASSIGNMENT

In assigning work, you as the supervisor should assign to each person jobs that are similar in nature. An employee who is assigned too many different types of jobs will waste time in going from one kind of work to another. It takes time for him to get to top production in one kind of task and, before he does so, he has to start on another.
When you assign work to people, remember that:

A. Job duties should be definite. Make it clear from the beginning what they are to do, how they are to do it, and why they are to do it. Let them know how much they are expected to do and how well they are expected to do it.
B. Check your assignments to be certain that there are no workers with too many unrelated duties, and that no two people have been given overlapping responsibilities. Your aim should be to have every task assigned to a specific person with the work fairly distributed and with each person doing his part.

IV. ASSIGNMENT OF RESPONSIBILITY AND DELEGATION OF AUTHORITY

A supervisor cannot delegate his final responsibility for the work of his department. The experienced supervisor knows that he gets his work done through people. He can't do it all himself. So he must assign the work and the responsibility for the work to his employees. Then they must be given the authority to carry out their responsibilities.

By assigning responsibility and delegating authority to carry out the responsibility, the supervisor builds in his workers initiative, resourcefulness, enthusiasm, and interest in their work. He is treating them as responsible adults. They can find satisfaction in their work, and they will respect the supervisor and be loyal to the supervisor.

PRINCIPLES OF ORGANIZATION

I. DEFINITION

Organization is the method of dividing up the work to provide the best channels for coordinated effort to get the agency's mission accomplished.

II. PURPOSE OF ORGANIZATION

A. To enable each employee within the organization to clearly know his responsibilities and relationships to his fellow employees and to organizational units
B. To avoid conflicts of authority and overlapping of jurisdiction.
C. To ensure teamwork.

III. BASIC CONSIDERATIONS IIN ORGANIZATIONAL PLANNING

A. The basic plans and objectives of the agency should be determined, and the organizational structure should be adapted to carry out effectively such plans and objectives.
B. The organization should be built around the major functions of the agency and not individuals or groups of individuals.

C. The organization should be sufficiently flexible to meet new and changing conditions which may be brought about from within or outside the department.
D. The organizational structure should be as simple as possible and the number of organizational units kept at a minimum.
E. The number of levels of authority should be kept at a minimum. Each additional management level lengthens the chain of authority and responsibility and increases the time for instructions to be distributed to operating levels and for decisions to be obtained from higher authority.
F. The form of organization should permit each executive to exercise maximum initiative within the limits of delegated authority.

IV. BASES FOR ORGANIZATION

A. Purpose (Examples: education, police, sanitation)
B. Process (Examples: accounting, legal, purchasing)
C. Clientele (Examples: welfare, parks, veteran)
D. Geographic (Examples: borough offices, precincts, libraries)

V. ASSIGNMENTS OF FUNCTIONS

A. Every function of the agency should be assigned to a specific organizational unit. Under normal circumstances, no single function should be assigned to more than one organizational unit.
B. There should be no overlapping, duplication, or conflict between organizational elements.
C. Line functions should be separated from staff functions, and proper emphasis should be placed on staff activities.
D. Functions which are closely related or similar should normally be assigned to a single organizational unit.
E. Functions should be properly distributed to promote balance, and to avoid overemphasis of less important functions and underemphasis of more essential functions.

VI. DELEGATION OF AUTHORITY AND RESPONSIBILITY

A. Responsibilities assigned to a specific individual or organizational unit should carry corresponding authority, and all statements of authority or limitations thereof should be as specific as possible.
B. Authority and responsibility for action should be decentralized to organizational units and individuals responsible for actual performance to the greatest extent possible, without relaxing necessary control over policy or the standardization of procedures. Delegation of authority will be consistent with decentralization of responsibility but such delegation will not divest an executive in higher authority of his overall responsibility.
C. The heads of organizational units should concern themselves with important matters and should delegate to the maximum extent details and routines performed in the ordinary course of business.
D. All responsibilities, authorities, and relationships should be stated in simple language to avoid misinterpretation.
E. Each individual or organizational unit charged with a specific responsibility will be held responsible for results.

VII. EMPLOYEE RELATIONSHIPS

A. The employees reporting to one executive should not exceed the number which can be effectively directed and coordinated. The number will depend largely upon the scope and extent of the responsibilities of the subordinates.
B. No person should report to more than one supervisor. Every supervisor should know who reports to him, and every employee should know to whom he reports. Channels of authority and responsibility should not be violated by staff units.
C. Relationships between organizational units within the agency and with outside organizations and associations should be clearly stated and thoroughly understood to avoid misunderstanding.

DELEGATING

I. WHAT IS DELEGATING?
Delegating is assigning a job to an employee, giving him the authority to get that job done, and giving him the responsibility for seeing to it that the job is done.

A. What To Delegate
1. Routine details
2. Jobs which may be necessary and take a lot of time, but do not have to be done by the supervisor personally (preparing reports, attending meetings, etc.)
3. Routine decision-making (making decisions which do not require the supervisor's personal attention)

B. What Not To Delegate
1. Job details which are *executive functions* (setting goals, organizing employees into a good team, analyzing results so as to plan for the future)
2. Disciplinary power (handling grievances, preparing service ratings, reprimands, etc.)
3. Decision-making which involves large numbers of employees or other bureaus and departments
4. Final and complete responsibility for the job done by the unit being supervised

C. Why Delegate?
1. To strengthen the organization by developing a greater number of skilled employees
2. To improve the employee's performance by giving him the chance to learn more about the job, handle some responsibility, and become more interested in getting the job done
3. To improve a supervisor's performance by relieving him of routine jobs and giving him more time for *executive functions* (planning, organizing, controlling, etc.) which cannot be delegated

II. TO WHOM TO DELEGATE
People with abilities not being used. Selection should be based on ability, not on favoritism.

REPORTS

I. DEFINITION

A report is an orderly presentation of factual information directed to a specific reader for a specific purpose

II. PURPOSE

The general purpose of a report is to bring to the reader useful and factual information about a condition or a problem. Some specific purposes of a report may be:

A. To enable the reader to appraise the efficiency or effectiveness of a person or an operation
B. To provide a basis for establishing standards
C. To reflect the results of expenditures of time, effort, and money
D. To provide a basis for developing or altering programs

III. TYPES

A. Information Report: Contains facts arranged in sequence
B. Summary (Examination) Report: Contains facts plus an analysis or discussion of the significance of the facts. Analysis may give advantages and disadvantages or give qualitative and quantitative comparisons
C. Recommendation Report: Contains facts, analysis, and conclusion logically drawn from the facts and analysis, plus a recommendation based upon the facts, analysis, and conclusions

IV. FACTORS TO CONSIDER BEFORE WRITING REPORT

A. Why write the report?: The purpose of the report should be clearly defined.
B. Who will read the report?: What level of language should be used? Will the reader understand professional or technical language?
C. What should be said?: What does the reader need or want to know about the subject?
D. How should it be said?: Should the subject be presented tactfully? Convincingly? In a stimulating manner?

V. PREPARATORY STEPS

A. Assemble the facts: Find out who, why, what, where, when, and how.
B. Organize the facts: Eliminate unnecessary information
C. Prepare an outline: Check for orderliness, logical sequence
D. Prepare a draft: Check for correctness, clearness, completeness, conciseness, and tone
E. Prepare it in final form: Check for grammar, punctuation, appearance

VI. OUTLINE FOR A RECOMMENDATION REPORT

Is the report:
A. Correct in information, grammar, and tone?
B. Clear?
C. Complete?

D. Concise?
E. Timely?
F. Worth its cost?

Will the report accomplish its purpose?

MANAGEMENT CONTROLS

I. CONTROL
What is control? What is controlled? Who controls?

The essence of control is action which adjusts operations to predetermined standards, and its basis is information in the hands of managers. Control is checking to determine whether plans are being observed and suitable progress toward stated objectives is being made, and action is taken, if necessary, to correct deviations.

We have a ready-made model for this concept of control in the automatic systems which are widely used for process control in the chemical land petroleum industries. A process control system works this way. Suppose, for example, it is desired to maintain a constant rate of flow of oil through a pipe at a predetermined or set-point value. A signal, whose strength represents the rate of flow, can be produced in a measuring device and transmitted to a control mechanism. The control mechanism, when it detects any deviation of the actual from the set-point signal, will reposition the value regulating flow rate.

II. BASIS FOR CONTROL

A process control mechanism thus acts to adjust operations to predetermined standards and does so on the basis of information it receives. In a parallel way, information reaching a manager gives him the opportunity for corrective action and is his basis for control. He cannot exercise control without such information, and he cannot do a complete job of managing without controlling.

III. POLICY

What is policy?

Policy is simply a statement of an organization's intention to act in certain ways when specified types of circumstances arise. It represents a general decision, predetermined and expressed as a principle or rule, establishing a normal pattern of conduct for dealing with given types of business events—usually recurrent. A statement is therefore useful in economizing the time of managers and in assisting them to discharge their responsibilities equitably and consistently.

Policy is not a means of control, but policy does generate the need for control.

Adherence to policies is not guaranteed nor can it be taken on faith. It has to be verified. Without verification, there is no basis for control. Policy and procedures, although closely related and interdependent to a certain extent, are not synonymous. A policy may be adopted, for example, to maintain a materials inventory not to exceed one million dollars.

A procedure for inventory control could interpret that policy and convert it into methods for keeping within that limit, with consideration, too, of possible but foreseeable expedient deviation.

IV. PROCEDURE

What is procedure?

A procedure specifically prescribes:

A. What work is to be performed by the various participants
B. Who are the respective participants
C. When and where the various steps in the different processes are to be performed
D. The sequence of operations that will insure uniform handling of recurring transactions
E. The paper that is involved, its origin, transition, and disposition

Necessary appurtenances to a procedure are:

A. Detailed organizational chart
B. Flow charts
C. Exhibits of forms, all presented in close proximity to the text of the procedure

V. BASIS OF CONTROL – INFORMATION IN THE HANDS OF MANAGERS

If the basis of control is information in the hands of managers, then reporting is elevated to a level of very considerable importance.

Types of reporting may include:

A. Special reports and routine reports
B. Written, oral, and graphic reports
C. Staff meetings
D. Conferences
E. Television screens
F. Non-receipt of information, as where management is by exception
G. Any other means whereby information is transmitted to a manager as a basis for control action

FRAMEWORK OF MANAGEMENT

I. ELEMENTS

A. Policy: It has to be verified, controlled.

B. Organization is part of the giving of an assignment. The organizational chart gives to each individual in his title, a first approximation of the nature of his assignment and orients him as being accountable to a certain individual. Organization is not in a true sense a means of control. Control is checking to ascertain whether the assignment is executed as intended and acting on the basis of that information.

C. Budgets perform three functions:
   1. They present the objectives, plans, and programs of the organization in financial terms.

2. They report the progress of actual performance against these predetermined objectives, plans, and programs.
3. Like organizational charts, delegations of authority, procedures, and job descriptions, they define the assignments which have flowed from the Chief Executive. Budgets are a means of control in the respect that they report progress of actual performance against the program. They provide information which enables managers to take action directed toward bringing actual results into conformity with the program.

D. Internal Check provides in practice for the principle that the same person should not have responsibility for all phases of a transaction. This makes it clearly an aspect of organization rather than of control. Internal Check is static, or built-in.

E. Plans, Programs, Objectives
People must know what they are trying to do. Objectives fulfill this need. Without them, people may work industriously and yet, working aimlessly, accomplish little. Plans and Programs complement Objectives, since they propose how and according to what time schedule the objectives are to be reached.

F. Delegations of Authority
Among the ways we have for supplementing the titles and lines of authority of an organizational chart are delegations of authority. Delegations of authority clarify the extent of authority of individuals and in that way serve to define assignments. That they are not means of control is apparent from the very fact that wherever there has been a delegation of authority, the need for control increases. This could hardly be expected to happen if delegations of authority were themselves means of control.

II. MANAGER'S RESPONSIBILITY

Control becomes necessary whenever a manager delegates authority to a subordinate because he cannot delegate and then simply sit back and forget4 about it. A manager's accountability to his own superior has not diminished one whit as a result of delegating part of his authority to a subordinate. The manager must exercise control over actions taken under the authority so delegated. That means checking serves as a basis for possible corrective action.

Objectives, plans, programs, organizational charts, and other elements of the managerial system are not fruitfully regarded as either controls or means of control. They are pre-established standards or models of performance to which operations are adjusted by the exercise of management control. These standards or models of performance are dynamic in character for they are constantly altered, modified, or revised. Policies, organizational set-up, procedures, delegations, etc. are constantly altered but, like objectives and plans, they remain in force until they are either abandoned or revised. All of the elements (or standards or models of performance), objectives, plans, and programs, policies, organization, etc. can be regarded as a *framework of management*.

III. CONTROL TECHNIQUES

Examples of control techniques:

A. Compare against established standards
B. Compare with a similar operation
C. Compare with past operations
D. Compare with predictions of accomplishment

IV. WHERE FORECASTS FIT

Control is after-the-fact while forecasts are before. Forecasts and projections are important for setting objectives and formulating plans.

Information for aiming and planning does not have to be before-the-fact. It may be an after-the-fact analysis proving that a certain policy has been impolitic in its effect on the relation of the company or department with customer, employee, taxpayer, or stockholder; or that a certain plan is no longer practical, or that a certain procedure is unworkable.

The prescription here certainly would not be in control (in these cases, control would simply bring operations into conformity with obsolete standards) but the establishment of new standards, a new policy, a new plan, and a new procedure to be controlled too.

Information is, of course, the basis for all communication in addition to furnishing evidence to management of the need for reconstructing the framework of management.

PROBLEM SOLVING

The accepted concept in modern management for problem solving is the utilization of the following steps:

A. Identify the problem
B. Gather data
C. List possible solutions
D. Test possible solutions
E. Select the best solution
F. Put the solution into actual practice

Occasions might arise where you would have to apply the second step of gathering data before completing the first step.

You might also find that it will be necessary to work on several steps at the same time.

I. IDENTIFY THE PROBLEM

Your first step is to define as precisely as possible the problem to be solved. While this may sound easy, it is often the most difficult part of the process.

It has been said of problem solving that you are halfway to the solution when you can write out a clear statement of the problem itself.

Our job now is to get below the surface manifestations of the trouble and pinpoint the problem. This is usually accomplished by a logical analysis, by going from the general to the particular; from the obvious to the not-so-obvious cause.

Let us say that production is behind schedule. WHY? Absenteeism is high. Now, is absenteeism the basic problem to be tackled, or is it merely a symptom of low morale among the workforce? Under these circumstances, you may decide that production is not the problem; the problem is *employee morale*.

In trying to define the problem, remember there is seldom one simple reason why production is lagging, or reports are late, etc.

Analysis usually leads to the discovery that an apparent problem is really made up of several subproblems which must be attacked separately.

Another way is to limit the problem, and thereby ease the task of finding a solution, and concentrate on the elements which are within the scope of your control.

When you have gone this far, write out a tentative statement of the problem to be solved.

II. GATHER DATA

In the second step, you must set out to collect all the information that might have a bearing on the problem. Do not settle for an assumption when reasonable fact and figures are available.

If you merely go through the motions of problem-solving, you will probably shortcut the information-gathering step. Therefore, do not stack the evidence by confining your research to your own preconceived ideas.

As you collect facts, organize them in some form that helps you make sense of them and spot possible relationships between them. For example, plotting cost per unit figures on a graph can be more meaningful than a long column of figures.

Evaluate each item as you go along. Is the source material absolutely, reliable, probably reliable, or not to be trusted.

One of the best methods for gathering data is to go out and look the situation over carefully. Talk to the people on the job who are most affected by this problem.

Always keep in mind that a primary source is usually better than a secondary source of information.

III. LIST POSSIBLE SOLUTIONS

This is the creative thinking step of problem solving. This is a good time to bring into play whatever techniques of group dynamics the agency or bureau might have developed for a joint attack on problems.

Now the important thing for you to do is: Keep an open mind. Let your imagination roam freely over the facts you have collected. Jot down every possible solution that occurs to you. Resist the temptation to evaluate various proposals as you go along. List seemingly absurd ideas along with more plausible ones. The more possibilities you list during this step, the less risk you will run of settling for merely a workable, rather than the best, solution.

Keep studying the data as long as there seems to be any chance of deriving additional ideas, solutions, explanations, or patterns from it.

IV. TEST POSSIBLE SOLUTIONS

Now you begin to evaluate the possible solutions. Take pains to be objective. Up to this point, you have suspended judgment but you might be tempted to select a solution you secretly favored all along and proclaim it as the best of the lot.

The secret of objectivity in this phase is to test the possible solutions separately, measuring each against a common yardstick. To make this yardstick try to enumerate as many specific criteria as you can think of. Criteria are best phrased as questions which you ask of each possible solution. They can be drawn from these general categories:

Suitability – Will this solution do the job?
Will it solve the problem completely or partially?
Is it a permanent or a stopgap solution?

Feasibility - Will this plan work in actual practice?
Can we afford this approach?
How much will it cost?

Acceptability - Will the boss go along with the changes required in the plan?
Are we trying to drive a tack with a sledge hammer?

V. SELECT THE BEST SOLUTION

This is the area of executive decision.

Occasionally, one clearly superior solution will stand out at the conclusion of the testing process. But often it is not that simple. You may find that no one solution has come through all the tests with flying colors.

You may also find that a proposal, which flunked miserably on one of the essential tests, racked up a very high score on others.

The best solution frequently will turn out to be a combination.

Try to arrange a marriage that will bring together the strong points of one possible solution with the particular virtues of another. The more skill and imagination that you apply, the greater is the likelihood that you will come out with a solution that is not merely adequate and workable, but is the best possible under the circumstances.

VI. PUT THE SOLUTION INTO ACTUAL PRACTICE

As every executive knows, a plan which works perfectly on paper may develop all sorts of bugs when put into actual practice.

Problem-solving does not stop with selecting the solution which looks best in theory. The next step is to put the chosen solution into action and watch the results. The results may point towards modifications.

If the problem disappears when you put your solution into effect, you know you have the right solution.

If it does not disappear, even after you have adjusted your plan to cover unforeseen difficulties that turned up in practice, work your way back through the problem-solving solutions.

Would one of them have worked better?
Did you overlook some vital piece of data which would have given you a different slant on the whole situation? Did you apply all necessary criteria in testing solutions? If no light dawns after this much rechecking, it is a pretty good bet that you defined the problem incorrectly in the first place.

You came up with the wrong solution because you tackled the wrong problem.

Thus, step six may become step one of a new problem-solving cycle.

COMMUNICATION

I. WHAT IS COMMUNICATION?

We communicate through writing, speaking, action, or inaction. In speaking to people face-to-face, there is opportunity to judge reactions and to adjust the message. This makes the supervisory chain one of the most, and in many instances the most, important channels of communication.

In an organization, communication means keeping employees informed about the organization's objectives, policies, problems, and progress. Communication is the free interchange of information, ideas, and desirable attitudes between and among employees and between employees and management.

II. WHY IS COMMUNICATION NEEDED?

A. People have certain social needs
B. Good communication is essential in meeting those social needs
C. While people have similar basic needs, at the same time they differ from each other
D. Communication must be adapted to these individual differences

An employee cannot do his best work unless he knows why he is doing it. If he has the feeling that he is being kept in the dark about what is going on, his enthusiasm and productivity suffer.

Effective communication is needed in an organization so that employees will understand what the organization is trying to accomplish; and how the work of one unit contributes to or affects the work of other units in the organization and other organizations.

III. HOW IS COMMUNICATION ACHIEVED?

Communication flows downward, upward, sideways.

A. Communication may come from top management down to employees. This is downward communication.

   Some means of downward communication are:
   1. Training (orientation, job instruction, supervision, public relations, etc.)
   2. Conferences
   3. Staff meetings
   4. Policy statements
   5. Bulletins
   6. Newsletters
   7. Memoranda
   8. Circulation of important letters

   In downward communication, it is important that employees be informed in advance of changes that will affect them.

B. Communications should also be developed so that the ideas, suggestions, and knowledge of employees will flow upward to top management.

   Some means of upward communication are:
   1. Personal discussion conferences
   2. Committees
   3. Memoranda
   4. Employees suggestion program
   5. Questionnaires to be filled in giving comments and suggestions about proposed actions that will affect field operations.

   Upward communication requires that management be willing to listen, to accept, and to make changes when good ideas are present. Upward communication succeeds when there is no fear of punishment for speaking out or lack of interest at the top. Employees will share their knowledge and ideas with management when interest is shown and recognition is given.

C. The advantages of downward communication:
   1. It enables the passing down of orders, policies, and plans necessary to the continued operation of the station.
   2. By making information available, it diminishes the fears and suspicions which result from misinformation and misunderstanding.
   3. It fosters the pride people want to have in their work when they are told of good work.
   4. It improves the morale and stature of the individual to be *in the know*.

5. It helps employees to understand, accept, and cooperate with changes when they know about them in advance.

D. The advantages of upward communication:
   1. It enables the passing upward of information, attitudes, and feelings.
   2. It makes it easier to find out how ready people are to receive downward communication.
   3. It reveals the degree to which the downward communication is understood and accepted.
   4. It helps to satisfy the basic social needs.
   5. It stimulates employees to participate in the operation of their organization.
   6. It encourage employees to contribute ideas for improving the efficiency and economy of operations.
   7. It helps to solve problem situations before they reach the explosion point.

IV. WHY DOES COMMUNICATION FAIL?

A. The technical difficulties of conveying information clearly
B. The emotional content of communication which prevents complete transmission
C. The fact that there is a difference between what management needs to say, what it wants to day, and what it does say
D. The fact that there is a difference between what employees would like to say, what they think is profitable or safe to say, and what they do say

V. HOW TO IMPROVE COMMUNICATION

As a supervisor, you are a key figure in communication. To improve as a communicator, you should:

A. Know: Knowing your subordinates will help you to recognize and work with individual differences.
B. Like: If you like those who work for you and those for whom you work, this will foster the kind of friendly, warm, work atmosphere that will facilitate communication.
C. Trust: Showing a sincere desire to communicate will help to develop the mutual trust and confidence which are essential to the free flow of communication.
D. Tell: Tell your subordinates and superiors *what's doing*. Tell your subordinates *why* as well as *how*.
E. Listen: By listening, you help others to talk and you create good listeners. Don't forget that listening implies action.
F. Stimulate: Communication has to be stimulated and encouraged. Be receptive to ideas and suggestions and motivate your people so that each member of the team identifies himself with the job at hand.
G. Consult: The most effective way of consulting is to let your people participate, insofar as possible, in developing determinations which affect them or their work.

VI. HOW TO DETERMINE WHETHER YOU ARE GETTING ACROSS

A. Check to see that communication is received and understood
B. Judge this understanding by actions rather than words
C. Adapt or vary communication, when necessary
D. Remember that good communication cannot cure all problems

VII. THE KEY ATTITUDE

Try to see things from the other person's point of view. By doing this, you help to develop the permissive atmosphere and the shared confidence and understanding which are essential to effective two-way communication.

Communication is a two-way process:

A. The basic purpose of any communication is to get action.
B. The only way to get action is through acceptance.
C. In order to get acceptance, communication must be humanly satisfying as well as technically efficient.

HOW ORDERS AND INSTRUCTIONS SHOULD BE GIVEN

I. CHARACTERISTICS OF GOOD ORDERS AND INSTRUCTIONS

A. Clear
Orders should be definite as to
—What is to be done
—Who is to do it
—When it is to be done
—Where it is to be done
—How it is to be done

B. Concise
Avoid wordiness. Orders should be brief and to the point.

C. Timely
Instructions and orders should be sent out at the proper time and not too long in advance of expected performance.

D. Possibility of Performance
Orders should be feasible:
1. Investigate before giving orders
2. Consult those who are to carry out instructions before formulating and issuing them

E. Properly Directed
Give the orders to the people concerned. Do not send orders to people who are not concerned. People who continually receive instructions that are not applicable to them get in the habit of neglecting instructions generally.

F. Reviewed Before Issuance
Orders should be reviewed before issuance:
1. Test them by putting yourself in the position of the recipient
2. If they involve new procedures, have the persons who are to do the work review them for suggestions.

G. Reviewed After Issuance
Persons who receive orders should be allowed to raise questions and to point out unforeseen consequences of orders.

H. Coordinated
Orders should be coordinated so that work runs smoothly.

I. Courteous
Make a request rather than a demand. There is no need to continually call attention to the fact that you are the boss.

J. Recognizable as an Order
Be sure that the order is recognizable as such.

K. Complete
Be sure recipient has knowledge and experience sufficient to carry out order. Give illustrations and examples.

A DEPARTMENTAL PERSONNEL OFFICE IS RESPONSIBLE FOR THE FOLLOWING FUNCTIONS

1. Policy
2. Personnel Programs
3. Recruitment and Placement
4. Position Classification
5. Salary and Wage Administration
6. Employee performance Standards and Evaluation
7. Employee Relations
8. Disciplinary Actions and Separations
9. Health and Safety
10. Staff Training and Development
11. Personnel Records, Procedures, and Reports
12. Employee Services
13. Personnel Research

SUPERVISION

I. LEADERSHIP

All leadership is based essentially on authority. This comes from two sources: It is received from higher management or it is earned by the supervisor through his methods of supervision. Although effective leadership has always depended upon the leader's using his authority in such a way as to appeal successfully to the motives of the people supervised, the conditions for making this appeal are continually changing. The key to today's problem of leadership is flexibility and resourcefulness on the part of the leader in meeting changes in conditions as they occur.

Three basic approaches to leadership are generally recognized:

A. The Authoritarian Approach
   1. The methods and techniques used in this approach emphasize the *I* in leadership and depend primarily on the formal authority of the leader. This authority is sometimes exercised in a hardboiled manner and sometimes in a benevolent

manner, but in either case the dominating role of the leader is reflected in the thinking, planning, and decisions of the group.

2. Group results are to a large degree dependent on close supervision by the leader. Usually, the individuals in the group will not show a high degree of initiative or acceptance of responsibility and their capacity to grow and develop probably will not be fully utilized. The group may react with resentment or submission, depending upon the manner and skill of the leader in using his authority.
3. This approach develops as a natural outgrowth of the authority that goes with the leader's job and his feeling of sole responsibility for getting the job done. It is relatively easy to use and does not require must resourcefulness.
4. The use of this approach is effective in times of emergencies, in meeting close deadline as a final resort, in settling some issues, in disciplinary matters, and with dependent individuals and groups.

B. The Laissez-Faire or Let 'em Alone Approach

1. This approach generally is characterized by an avoidance of leadership responsibility by the leader. The activities of the group depend largely on the choice of its members rather than the leader.
2. Group results probably will be poor. Generally, there will be disagreements over petty things, bickering, and confusion. Except for a few aggressive people, individuals will not show much initiative and growth and development will be retarded. There may be a tendency for informal leaders to take over leadership of the group.
3. This approach frequently results from the leader's dislike of responsibility, from his lack of confidence, from failure of other methods to work, from disappointment or criticism. It is usually the easiest of the three to use and requires both understanding and resourcefulness on the part of the leader.
4. This approach is occasionally useful and effective, particularly in forcing dependent individuals or groups to rely on themselves, to give someone a chance to save face by clearing his own difficulties, or when action should be delayed temporarily for good cause.

C. The Democratic Approach

1. The methods and techniques used in this approach emphasize the *we* in leadership and build up the responsibility of the group to attain its objectives. Reliance is placed largely on the earned authority of the leader.
2. Group results are likely to be good because most of the job motives of the people will be satisfied. Cooperation and teamwork, initiative, acceptance of responsibility, and the individual's capacity for growth probably will show a high degree of development.
3. This approach grows out of a desire or necessity of the leader to find ways to appeal effectively to the motivation of his group. It is the best approach to build up inside the person a strong desire to cooperate and apply himself to the job. It is the most difficult to develop, and requires both understanding and resourcefulness on the part of the leader.
4. The value of this approach increases over a long period where sustained efficiency and development of people are important. It may not be fully effective in all situations, however, particularly when there is not sufficient time to use it properly or where quick decisions must be made.

All three approaches are used by most leaders and have a place in supervising people. The extent of their use varies with individual leaders, with some using one approach predominantly. The leader who uses these three approaches, and varies their use with time and circumstance, is probably the most effective. Leadership which is used predominantly with a democratic approach requires more resourcefulness on the part of the leader but offers the greatest possibilities in terms of teamwork and cooperation.

The one best way of developing democratic leadership is to provide a real sense of participation on the part of the group, since this satisfies most of the chief job motives. Although there are many ways of providing participation, consulting as frequently as possible with individuals and groups on things that affect them seems to offer the most in building cooperation and responsibility. Consultation takes different forms, but it is most constructive when people feel they are actually helping in finding the answers to the problems on the job.

There are some requirements of leaders in respect to human relations which should be considered in their selection and development. Generally, the leader should be interested in working with other people, emotionally stable, self-confident, and sensitive to the reactions of others. In addition, his viewpoint should be one of getting the job done through people who work cooperatively in response to his leadership. He should have a knowledge of individual and group behavior, but, most important of all, he should work to combine all of these requirements into a definite, practical skill in leadership.

II. NINE POINTS OF CONTRAST BETWEEN *BOSS* AND *LEADER*

A. The boss drives his men; the leader coaches them.
B. The boss depends on authority; the leader on good will.
C. The boss inspires fear; the leader inspires enthusiasm.
D. The boss says I; the leader says *We*.
E. The boss says *Get here on time*; the leader gets there ahead of time.
F. The boss fixes the blame for the breakdown; the leader fixes the breakdown.
G. The boss knows how it is done; the leader shows how.
H. The boss makes work a drudgery; the leader makes work a game.
I. The boss says *Go*; the leader says *Let's go*.

EMPLOYEE MORALE

Employee morale is the way employees feel about each other, the organization or unit in which they work, and the work they perform.

I. SOME WAYS TO DEVELOP AND MAINTAIN GOOD EMPLYEE MORALE

A. Give adequate credit and praise when due.
B. Recognize importance of all jobs and equalize load with proper assignments, always giving consideration to personality differences and abilities.
C. Welcome suggestions and do not have an *all-wise* attitude. Request employees' assistance in solving problems and use assistants when conducting group meetings on certain subjects.
D. Properly assign responsibilities and give adequate authority for fulfillment of such assignments.

E. Keep employees informed about matters that affect them.
F. Criticize and reprimand employees privately.
G. Be accessible and willing to listen.
H. Be fair.
I. Be alert to detect training possibilities so that you will not miss an opportunity to help each employee do a better job, and if possible with less effort on his part.
J. Set a good example.
K. Apply the golden rule.

II. SOME INDICATIONS OF GOOD MORALE

A. Good quality of work
B. Good quantity
C. Good attitude of employees
D. Good discipline
E. Teamwork
F. Good attendance
G. Employee participation

MOTIVATION

DRIVES

A drive, stated simply, is a desire or force which causes a person to do or say certain things. These are some of the most usual drives and some of their identifying characteristics recognizable in people motivated by such drives:

A. Security (desire to provide for the future)
Always on time for work
Works for the same employer for many years
Never takes unnecessary chances
Seldom resists doing what he is told

B. Recognition (desire to be rewarded for accomplishment)
Likes to be asked for his opinion
Becomes very disturbed when he makes a mistake
Does things to attract attention
Likes to see his name in print

C. Position (desire to hold certain status in relation to others)
Boasts about important people he knows
Wants to be known as a key man
Likes titles
Demands respect
Belongs to clubs, for prestige

D. Accomplishment (desire to get things done)
Complains when things are held up
Likes to do things that have tangible results
Never lies down on the job
Is proud of turning out good work

E. Companionship (desire to associate with other people)
Likes to work with others
Tells stories and jokes
Indulges in horseplay
Finds excuses to talk to others on the job

F. Possession (desire to collect and hoard objects)
Likes to collect things
Puts his name on things belonging to him
Insists on the same location

Supervisors may find that identifying the drives of employees is a helpful step toward motivating them to self-improvement and better job performance. For example: An employee's job performance is below average. His supervisor, having previously determined that the employee is motivated by a drive for security, suggests that taking training courses will help the employee to improve, advance, and earn more money. Since earning more money can be a step toward greater security, the employee's drive for security would motivate him to take the training suggested by the supervisor. In essence, this is the process of charting an employee's future course by using his motivating drives to positive advantage.

EMPLOYEE PARTICIPATION

I. WHAT IS PARTICIPATION

Employee participation is the employee's giving freely of his time, skill, and knowledge to an extent which cannot be obtained by demand.

II. WHY IS IT IMPORTANT?

The supervisor's responsibility is to get the job done through people. A good supervisor gets the job done through people who work willingly and well. The participation of employees is important because:

A. Employees develop a greater sense of responsibility when they share in working out operating plans and goals.
B. Participation provides greater opportunity and stimulation for employees to learn, and to develop their ability.
C. Participation sometimes provides better solutions to problems because such solutions may combine the experience and knowledge of interested employees who want the solutions to work.
D. An employee or group may offer a solution which the supervisor might hesitate to make for fear of demanding too much.

E. Since the group wants to make the solution work, they exert pressure in a constructive way on each other.
F. Participation usually results in reducing the need for close supervision.

II. HOW MAY SUPERVISORS OBTAIN IT?

Participation is encouraged when employees feel that they share some responsibility for the work and that their ideas are sincerely wanted and valued. Some ways of obtaining employee participation are:

A. Conduct orientation programs for new employees to inform them about the organization and their rights and responsibilities as employees.
B. Explain the aims and objectives of the agency. On a continuing basis, be sure that the employees know what these aims and objectives are.
C. Share job successes and responsibilities and give credit for success.
D. Consult with employees, both as individuals and in groups, about things that affect them.
E. Encourage suggestions for job improvements. Help employees to develop good suggestions. The suggestions can bring them recognition. The city's suggestion program offers additional encouragement through cash awards.

The supervisor who encourages employee participation is not surrendering his authority. He must still make decisions and initiate action, and he must continue to be ultimately responsible for the work of those he supervises. But, through employee participation, he is helping his group to develop greater ability and a sense of responsibility while getting the job done faster and better.

STEPS IN HANDLING A GRIEVANCE

1. Get the Facts
   a. Listen sympathetically
   b. Let him talk himself out
   c. Get his story straight
   d. Get his point of view
   e. Don't argue with him
   f. Give him plenty of time
   g. Conduct the interview privately
   h. Don't try to shift the blame or pass the buck

2. Consider the Facts
   a. Consider the employee's viewpoint
   b. How will the decision affect similar cases
   c. Consider each decision as a possible precedent
   d. Avoid snap judgments—don't jump to conclusions

3. Make or Get a Decision
   a. Frame an effective counter-proposal
   b. Make sure it is fair to all
   c. Have confidence in your judgment
   d. Be sure you can substantiate your decision

4. Notify the Employee of Your Decision
   Be sure he is told; try to convince him that the decision is fair and just.

5. Take Action When Needed and If Within Your Authority
   Otherwise, tell employee that the matter will be called to the attention of the proper person or that nothing can be done, and why it cannot.

6. Follow through to see that the desired result is achieved.

7. Record key facts concerning the complaint and the action taken.

8. Leave the way open to him to appeal your decision to a higher authority.

9. Report all grievances to your superior, whether they are appealed or not.

DISCIPLINE

Discipline is training that develops self-control, orderly conduct, and efficiency.

To discipline does not necessarily mean to punish.

To discipline does mean to train, to regulate, and to govern conduct.

I. THE DISCIPLINARY INTERVIEW

Most employees sincerely want to do what is expected of them. In other words, they are self-disciplined. Some employees, however, fail to observe established rules and standards, and disciplinary action by the supervisor is required.

The primary purpose of disciplinary action is to improve conduct without creating dissatisfaction, bitterness, or resentment in the process.

Constructive disciplinary action is more concerned with causes and explanations of breaches of conduct than with punishment. The disciplinary interview is held to get at the causes of apparent misbehavior and to motivate better performance in the future.

It is important that the interview be kept on an impersonal a basis as possible. If the supervisor lets the interview descend to the plane of an argument, it loses its effectiveness.

II. PLANNING THE INTERVIEW

Get all pertinent facts concerning the situation so that you can talk in specific terms to the employee.

Review the employee's record, appraisal ratings, etc.

Consider what you know about the temperament of the employee. Consider your attitude toward the employee. Remember that the primary requisite of disciplinary action is fairness.

Don't enter upon the interview when angry.

Schedule the interview for a place which is private and out of hearing of others.

III. CONDUCTING THE INTERVIEW

A. Make an effort to establish accord.
B. Question the employee about the apparent breach of discipline. Be sure that the question is not so worded as to be itself an accusation.
C. Give the employee a chance to tell his side of the story. Give him ample opportunity to talk.
D. Use understanding—listening except where it is necessary to ask a question or to point out some details of which the employee may not be aware. If the employee misrepresents facts, make a plain, accurate statement of the facts, but don't argue and don't engage in personal controversy.
E. Listen and try to understand the reasons for the employee's (mis)conduct. First of all, don't assume that there has been a breach of discipline. Evaluate the employee's reasons for his conduct in the light of his opinions and feelings concerning the consistency and reasonableness of the standards which he was expected to follow. Has the supervisor done his part in explaining the reasons for the rule? Was the employee's behavior unintentional or deliberate? Does he think he had real reasons for his actions? What new facts is he telling? Do the facts justify his actions? What causes, other than those mentioned, could have stimulated the behavior?
F. After listening to the employee's version of the situation, and if censure of his actions is warranted, the supervisor should proceed with whatever criticism is justified. Emphasis should be placed on future improvement rather than exclusively on the employee's failure to measure up to expected standards of job conduct.
G. Fit the criticism to the individual. With one employee, a word of correction may be all that is required.
H. Attempt to distinguish between unintentional error and deliberate misbehavior. An error due to ignorance requires training and not censure.
I. Administer criticism in a controlled, even tone of voice, never in anger. Make it clear that you are acting as an agent of the department. In general, criticism should refer to the job or the employee's actions and not to the person. Criticism of the employee's work is not an attack on the individual.
J. Be sure the interview does not destroy the employee's self-confidence. Mention his good qualities and assure him that you feel confident that he can improve his performance.
K. Wherever possible, before the employee leaves the interview, satisfy him that the incident is closed, that nothing more will be said on the subject unless the offense is repeated.

www.ingramcontent.com/pod-product-compliance
Lightning Source LLC
Chambersburg PA
CBHW081814300426
44116CB00014B/2357
9781799310792